Better than working

Better than working

Life behind the camera

Richard Hakin

AAVO

First published in 1999 by AAVO,
8 Edis Street, London NW1 8LG, UK
tel/fax 0171-722 9243
e-mail tottatv@aol.com

ISBN 0 9507582 4 8

Typeset by Dick Hammett
Cover illustration by Bryan Reading
Printed by Lontec, Borehamwood, Herts WD6 1JB

Acknowledgements

Mike Coles (cameraman) for all the work he's given me

Andy Elliot (cameraman) for giving me that vital first break into the industry

Penny Dance at Skillset and Nik Carnell at FT2 for the information on industry training

Sue Beeby at the Museum of Mankind for research services

Dr Jan Evans for advice for the section about ante-natal surgery

Michael Evans (computer whizz) for help with my computer

Harris Watts (publisher) for the editing and for pushing me to be better

My parents for allowing me not to become a chartered accountant

Richard Hakin

Born in Monkseaton, County Tyne and Wear. Raised and educated in the North-East before attending university at Sheffield. Left with an honours degree in accountancy, enabling him to land his first job as a stage hand at the Crucible Theatre, Sheffield. After a year shifting scenery he went to Bristol Old Vic Drama School to study stage management and then spent five years working for companies such as the Bristol Old Vic, the Royal Court and the Royal Shakespeare Company.

Entered the film industry in 1986 and has worked freelance ever since in documentaries, commercials, music videos, news, sport, light entertainment, feature films and television dramas, involving many trips to the Far East, Middle East, New Zealand, America and Europe. Began writing in 1995 and is currently working on a film screenplay.

Other books published by AAVO

On Camera
Essential Know-how for Programme-makers
Harris Watts (1997)
ISBN 0 9507582-3-X

Directing On Camera
A Checklist of Video and Film Technique
Harris Watts (1992)
ISBN 0 9507582-2-1

AAVO, 8 Edis Street, London NW1 8LG, UK
tel/fax 0171-722 9243
e-mail tottatv@aol.com

To my parents and Mary-Rose

Contents

Preface

The great danger of writing anything that even vaguely resembles an autobiography is that it can be seen as an enormous ego trip - and if you've never been famous or are never likely to be, then a pretty pointless trip at that.

So why write this? Why the enormous investment in time and effort? Why the bleary-eyed late nights spent staring at that damn cursor as it stubbornly refuses to punch out the next word?

Three reasons.

Firstly, I always seem to struggle with that question of modern social intercourse, 'So, what do you do then?' To anyone outside the film or television industry my job as a film camera assistant seems a total mystery. Whenever I try and explain it, the initial reaction 'Oh, that's interesting' is quickly enveloped in a mist of incomprehension. Perhaps this will make it all a little clearer.

Secondly, like ancient seafarers all film technicians have their store of tales, but given the closed and close-knit world of the film set, they are almost impossible to relate in a couple of sentences of casual conversation and so I wanted the chance to do them justice.

Finally, this is something of an extravagant personal diary. Given the ephemeral nature of my working lifestyle many of the jobs I've done were in danger of becoming nothing more than vague memories, ultimately to be lost forever. So this is my own piece of personal history.

Essentially I've tried to give a light-hearted, behind-the-scenes look at working in the film and television industry. Although film-making is a technical process I've kept the explanations fairly simple, yet hopefully revealed enough to give an insight into what it's like to be part of a film crew. To those colleagues who may mock the simplicity of my descriptions, just cast your minds back to when you first started and remember how little you knew. Everybody has been sufficiently intrigued at some point to ask, 'What's a Best Boy?' Answers on a postcard, please.

The animal kingdom

Ask any actor how they feel about working with kids and
animals and they usually grab the nearest two pieces of
timber, make a sign of the cross and utter a strangled cry of
'Begone!' For when it comes to upstaging and scene-
stealing, small children and the lower echelons of the food
chain are masters of all they survey. Not for nothing did
W. C. Fields remark 'Any man who hates children and small
dogs can't be all bad.'

Yet from a technical viewpoint, working with kids is
pretty straightforward. Thanks to a raft of children's drama
schools, miniature thespians can now display a frightening
degree of professionalism.

'So we start with the two-shot of me and Mum, come in
for my close-up and then go to the pack-shot of hands on the
product?' - this from a four-year-old cutie on a commercial
for dishwashing liquid.

Animals, however, are a different kettle of fish.

The programme *That's Life* always had a loopy animal story
to balance the more serious consumer aspects of the show.
The item usually involved an owner who was convinced that
their pet displayed genuine human qualities, and that it was
imperative that the whole world knew of this phenomenon.

Such as the lady from Manchester, Helen, who had
contacted the offices of *That's Life*, claiming that her dogs
could talk. A researcher went off to check out the story and
reported back that although the dogs growled and whined in
a variety of pitches, it was impossible to distinguish any
clear vocal sounds.

'Doesn't matter, we'll make something out of it', came
the reaction from London. So on this flimsy basis a director,
cameraman, camera assistant, sound recordist, electrician,
interviewer and production assistant were dispatched to
Manchester for the day to cover the story. (I thought you
might like to know where your licence fee goes.)

We arrived to be met by Robin, the director, whose attitude to the whole farce was very firmly tongue-in-cheek.

'I'm so lucky. Everyone in the office was fighting to get this one. This is really going to launch my career into the big time.'

As we started to bring the equipment into the lounge we were struck by the extensive display of china and porcelain hippopotami. They were everywhere: crowding mantelpieces, filling display cabinets, even a set of flying hippos on the wall. I've seen homes bearing tribute to dogs, cats, birds, horses and even frogs - but never hippos. It was a strange start to a strange day.

We continued setting up. At one end of the lounge was a large set of French windows but the sunlight was too bright. To diffuse the light, Brian, the electrician, started to cover the windows with large sheets of trace, a heavy-duty form of tracing paper.

Helen came into the room and let out a howl of protest.

'You can't do that - the gnomes won't be able to see in!'

'Er.. sorry, what?' asked Brian, caught off-guard.

'The gnomes. They'll feel left out if they can't see what's happening.'

At the foot of the window, looking in from the garden, were two plastic gnomes, their faces pressed against the glass.

This crisis was averted by Brian carefully cutting out a hole at the bottom of the trace, thus allowing the gnomes to happily view the day's proceedings.

Welcome to The Twilight Zone.

The stars of the show duly arrived, we were all introduced and immediately a canine discussion broke out concerning the effects of the Government's monetarist policy viz-a-viz inflation, unemployment and the exchange rate....

Helen cooed over her charges.

'Say "Mama"'

Silence.

'Say "I love Mama."'

'Ruff!'

'There! Did you hear it?' exclaimed Helen excitedly.

'Er....Mike, did you get that?' enquired Robin, passing the buck to our sound recordist.

Mike resisted stating the obvious.

'Er....I think so - but could I hear some more?'

This, in a nutshell, was the pattern for the day. Several hours later, having spent the entire morning with headphones clamped to his head and listening to nothing but doggy growls and whines, Mike had left Planet Earth far behind.

By mid-afternoon we were dredging new depths of banality. Helen and the dogs were still on the sofa, with Gavin (the interviewer) opposite them in a large armchair. Hiding behind the chair to avoid distracting the animals was Robin. I glanced down at him. He seemed to be in state of extreme distress, biting his hand and silently convulsing. The lunacy of the day had finally got to him. His hysteria became contagious and I too got the giggles. I bit my cheek, clamped my jaw and tried to recall the worst moments of my life but to no avail. I caught Mike's eye but he remained completely unaffected, probably now well on his way to Alpha Centauri.

The day mercifully ended and we started to pack away the gear.

At this point things got a little strange.

Helen's brother came downstairs eating a can of dog food while Helen started playing a porno video. Perhaps she thought that as we had all the camera gear handy.... We cleared out of the house in record time.

Several months later I saw the item on *That's Life*. Our sterling efforts to upstage David Attenborough and be the first to record canine speech appeared as a brief one-minute novelty piece at the end of the programme. But you know, if you listen carefully....

I can think of few things more risky than planning a film production around a performance from an animal, particularly if the animal in question has a bird-like brain (as most birds do).

I was working on a commercial that centred around a canary singing. Nothing more complicated than that. Just a close-up shot of a canary, sitting on its perch, in a cage, singing. Couldn't be simpler. After all, what are canaries famous for? What else do they do? If you want a bird that sings, you get a canary, right? I mean, what could possibly go wrong? We all expected an early finish to the day.

By the end of the one and only day planned for the job we hadn't had so much as a tweet. Not one. Zip.

That's not to say that the canary owner hadn't tried his best. He brought along cages of canaries, each of which was given its chance for stardom, each of which bounced happily back and forth along the perch, ate its millet, sharpened its beak on the cuttlebone, did GBH to the mirror, but categorically refused to sing.

'Maybe the studio is too hot.'

The studio was one of those cavernous sound stages at Elstree. Spielberg was later to use it for *Indiana Jones and the Last Crusade*. Using it for a canary seemed a slight case of overkill. The huge doors were rolled open.

Nothing.

'Maybe it's scared by the lights.'

It's a bit difficult to film without light, but the lamps were suitably adjusted to give a more subtle effect.

Nothing.

'Maybe it's scared by all the attention.'

We tried looking uninterested.

Nothing.

'Maybe there are too many people here.'

The enormous studio was immediately awarded Category A security closed-set status. Access forbidden to all but an essential few. A similar course is sometimes followed if a film involves a particularly intimate love scene. But this was for a canary.

Nothing.

The day progressed with more suggestions, each of which proved to be as fruitless as the last. It was decided to schedule an extra day's filming, with a new group of birds.

Day Two.

Nothing.

By now the producer was nearing the limits of both his budget and his patience. He confronted the canary owner.

'Do you realise these canaries are ruining my company?'

It's not easy to ask a question like that and retain your professional credibility.

A third day was scheduled, but this time at another location - a smaller, more intimate studio. It was a lovely day and while we were setting up, the studio doors were left open to let in the sunlight and fresh air.

The canary went berserk. Arias, ballads, heavy rock, requests even. We set up the camera and soon had the required shots. A major discovery had been made in the field of avian research. Canaries don't like being shut up in dark, hot, cavernous studios. Canaries like fresh air and sunlight.

Not a lot of people know that.

Notwithstanding logic and common sense, after several experiences I am now convinced that some animals know when they are being filmed and perform accordingly. The most startling evidence of this came during a day spent with the dolphins at Windsor Safari Park.

We were doing some filming for a children's television programme, the standard stuff about dolphins and how cute'n'clever they are. The day commenced with Stuart, the presenter, standing in front of the dolphin tank.

'I'm standing here in front of the dolphinarium at Windsor Safari Park....'

At this point, and unknown to Stuart, one of the dolphins swam down to see what was happening and hovered just behind Stuart's right shoulder, looking directly at him as if listening intently. Stuart continued for about a minute with the dolphin still apparently rapt in attention and completed his piece with the words, '...and we'll see why dolphins are regarded as the most intelligent animals on earth.' At this point the dolphin turned directly to camera, nodded vigorously several times and then swam off. As a display of anthropomorphism it was pure Disney.

We couldn't believe our luck at such a perfect shot and looked forward to seeing the item being broadcast. But tragically this was never to be, as the laboratory used the wrong processing chemicals, losing both the film and one of my strongest professional memories.

On another occasion, this time for Thames Television, we were interviewing the dolphin keeper on the poolside. Unaccustomed to not being the centre of attention the dolphins swam to the side, rose out of the water and starting nudging the tripod with their snouts, disrupting the shot.

'Must know you're a freelancer,' said the grip, a full-time employee with Thames, voicing the rivalry between freelancers and staff crew.

To distract the dolphins from further assaults I spent the interview rubbing the animals under their snouts, totally captivated (me, not them). I later tried the same with the Park's killer whale and nearly lost my hand.

While one can argue that dolphins are far too intelligent to be used as circus acts, anybody who has seen them in the wild will testify to their innate sense of fun and apparent desire to perform for an audience. I've watched them several times in the open sea and I always come away feeling envious of a lifestyle that seems to involve nothing more than sleeping, eating, having a few laughs and making little dolphins.

In its heyday London Zoo was internationally famous as one of the world's oldest and largest zoos, but perhaps less well known for its conservation and breeding programme. So the British Council commissioned a documentary to promote the zoo's work with threatened species, an activity that also generated a thriving export trade with overseas game parks.

The two weeks spent in Regent's Park and Whipsnade gave me a rare perspective of wildlife. Stalking wallabies across a large field with the keeper trying to dart a pregnant female to check on the state of its foetus made working on commercials for Whizzo soap powder seem slightly mundane - witness the following.

One thing you realise when working up close with large animals is the sheer power and strength that they possess. We were filming a vet who had to drug a female African water buffalo in order to check its readiness for mating. With great ceremony he drew a large syringe from his case.

'That's the tranquilliser?' I enquired, somewhat obviously.

'No, this is for me.' (Yea, right.)

He then prepared another syringe.

'This is for the animal.'

The tranquilliser needed to suppress the buffalo was several thousand times more powerful than morphine. If the vet accidentally injected himself in the risky process of trying to inject the animal, he would have just a couple of minutes to administer the antidote before death occurred. After several such deaths the procedure was adopted of preparing the antidote for the vet before the drug for the animal. It added a whole new meaning to 'safe drug habit'.

I once read that when attacking a human, a leopard will pin the victim down with its front paws while using the rear claws to disembowel. It's funny the thoughts that spring to mind when you find yourself inside an enclosure facing four pairs of black eyes only ten yards away. Much is made of the leopard's grace and beauty, but up close they looked like a bunch of muggers, lean and hungry. And I'm allergic to cats.

The keeper, director, cameraman and myself had all entered the enclosure with a supposedly nonchalant air. All that stuff about not showing fear. Complete rubbish, of course.

Yet to my immense surprise (and relief) we bluffed the leopards out. As we approached, they all scattered to the far end of the enclosure. Because the shot required a background devoid of wire or bars we had to try and entice the cats away from the fence and back towards us. Oh yes, wise move. But despite enticements of raw meat the four animals steadfastly refused to come any closer. They'd obviously realised that we were the real predators. So much for dumb animals.

Occasionally you meet someone whose name is a perfect match for their occupation. While this can be mildly amusing, we discovered someone who must not only have cursed his parents, but who also displayed a seemingly masochistic streak in his choice of career.

We were filming a herd of deer. Although the herd was a healthy size, for some reason best known to himself the stag wasn't mating with the does and so the females had to be artificially inseminated. The first step thus was to obtain the semen from the stag. This involved darting the stag and once unconscious, inserting an eighteen-inch black rod (no, not down its throat) through which a low voltage current was passed, stimulating the stag to ejaculate. Well... you would, wouldn't you.

The man in charge of this breeding programme was called Richard Kock.

I doubt if his friends called him Dick.

Couldn't his parents have named him something a little less obvious - like William or Roger?

Or Ivor.

If you use the term 'baby' to describe any animal you instantly conjure up an image of something cute, cuddly and harmless. Now a four-foot 'baby' elephant may indeed be cute, but cuddling one is almost impossible and harmless it certainly ain't, having the strength and will to do exactly as it pleases. Witness the incident in *Blue Peter* in 1969 when the keeper of a young elephant was unable to control either the animal or its bodily functions as it careered around the studio, ruining Val Singleton's slingbacks as she, Pete Purves and John Noakes gamely continued reading their autocues. The scene has become a television classic and is unashamedly revived at the slightest opportunity.

I mention that particular scene because we had a similar experience with the zoo's young jumbo. We were set up to do an 'up and past', i.e. the elephant is led up towards the camera and then continues past as the camera pans with it. To keep the area around the tripod clear, I placed my large padded accessories bag, containing spare magazines of film, lenses and tins of film stock, on the ground about thirty yards away.

The shot started well enough, the keeper walking towards the camera with the young elephant. Suddenly Dumbo took off at a gallop. He brushed past the camera, pulling the hapless keeper behind him. The reason for the animal's sudden bolt soon became clear: it had spotted my grey, elephant-coloured bag and wanted to investigate. It charged up to the bag containing fragile equipment worth thousands of pounds - and then stood on it.

'Stop that!' I yelled - as you do with an elephant.

No way. This was far too much fun. Stomp, stomp, kick.

I reached the bag as the keeper finally managed to haul back his young charge. Gingerly I unzipped the top, expecting to hear accompanying tinkling sounds.

To my amazement everything was still in one piece. I'm sure the manufacturers won't object to an unsolicited testimonial.

The Lowe Prowe Bag: Elephant Proof.

After a week or so at the zoo we began to appreciate the theory that an animal owner can reflect the disposition of their charge, and possibly vice versa. I'll spare you puns about the bouncy personality of the wallaby keeper, but generally the degree of aggression or placidity in the animal was reflected in the keeper.

So off we go to film the tigers. We stepped inside the building that housed the cages. True to form, the keeper snarled a welcome.

'I've got a bitch of an animal to deal with and she's in a bad mood today so you'd better do exactly as I say or you'll be in big trouble.'

We were standing next to the narrow transit cage that connected the tigers' individual pens to the outer enclosure. The bars were just wide enough for a tiger to slip a paw through, so two feet outside the cage was a white line.

'See that line? Put one foot over that and she'll ruin your day.'

Maybe his haemorrhoids were playing up, but to be fair to the keeper this was serious stuff. Guiding the big cats down this passage involved him opening and closing a series of gates, placing him dangerously close to these magnificent beasts. It was no job for a shrinking violet.

There were three tigers, including the one with the bad attitude we'd been warned about. Up to now, they'd remained hidden behind the walled pens, creating a greater sense of menace than if they'd been in full view. The door to the first pen clanged open. A huge streak of black and orange fur sped through the transit passage and out into the sunlight. The second tiger cruised by, giving us barely a cursory glance.

Then the third cage was opened.

A blur of spitting anger hissed from inside. She didn't want to come out and play. She'd much rather stay inside and shred a few humans. The keeper decided no more Mr Nice Guy. After much snarling (from both sides) our star was coaxed out of her den, claws slashing at the keeper through the bars, before finally being persuaded to go out and meet her public.

Far from ruining our day she had made it memorable in spectacular fashion.

I mentioned earlier that I am allergic to cats. While filming in Alexandria in Egypt I had an experience equivalent to dropping an agoraphobic into the middle of the Sahara.

We were in Egypt for a series on the Mediterranean and were driving around Alexandria looking for a high vantage point to capture the whole port and harbour scene. A local guide said that a flat belonging to a friend of hers had a balcony that could provide the view we were after.

We arrived at an apartment block and went up in the lift to recce the potential viewpoint. As the lift doors opened we noticed a strange smell. On opening the door to the flat the smell became an overpowering stench. In the gloom of the apartment were cats. Everywhere. Not just a few, but dozens. If Hitchcock had ever wanted to produce a feline follow-up to *The Birds* he would have needed to look no further. My allergy screamed red alert.

We tentatively entered the apartment, silently surveyed by a hundred pairs of eyes. We had to tread carefully as the floor was covered with piles of excrement. Breathing became an optional extra. The cats were not the only form of wildlife: nightmare cockroaches scuttled across the floor, over the furniture and up the walls. The sofa was housing a flea convention. The only consolation was that there were unlikely to be any rats. Otherwise it was the vilest place I had ever been in. George, our sound recordist, looked into one of the bedrooms and quickly retreated in disgust.

'You should see what's on one of the beds.'

If it was worse than what was currently on offer, I preferred to remain in blissful ignorance.

Walking among the cats was an unnerving experience. They remained completely motionless other than to turn their heads as we passed by. I began to appreciate the theme of Hitchcock's film, the sense of menace that can be created by large numbers of normally passive and generally harmless animals.

The old lady who owned the flat guided us through the filth towards the balcony. I know it's common for elderly ladies to keep a cat for company but this was beyond belief. No human could actually live in these conditions.

The view from the balcony was nothing like as promising as we had been lead to believe, and to my relief the director shelved any plans to film there. The prospect of carrying in equipment while dodging cat shit, fleas and cockroaches and then trying to work in the middle of a cesspit held little appeal.

Back in the street we quizzed our guide about the story behind the flat. The woman who owned the place was apparently famous as the Cat Lady Of Alexandria. She didn't actually live there herself but ran it as a cat sanctuary, while she lived in the apartment below. The number of feline occupants was kept to seventy-eight, no more, no less, but the significance of the unusual figure was never explained.

As we drove away I was tempted to ask George what he had actually seen on the bed, but decided against it. I still don't know.

To end this chapter on animal encounters, a scene of romantic nature at its most sublime. We were in the Camargue in southern France, hoping to film the region's famous white horses, but had been warned that this could be difficult due to their rather timid nature.

The plan was to rise early, surreptitiously set up a shot of one of the herds and then scare the horses off into a wild splashing gallop across the marshes, grey ghosts shrouded in the swirling morning mist. Cinematic perfection.

With due stealth we crept across a field and silently set up the camera. The herd was grazing some fifty yards away, still blissfully unaware. Everything was ready. The scene was perfect.

'And this year's BAFTA Award for Best Wildlife Film goes to....'

As the camera started rolling we all yelled and whooped at the top of our voices.

Nothing.

We tried again.

The horses ambled over to nuzzle both camera and crew.

Like I said, some animals just know when they're being filmed.

Hunting the Loch Ness Wellington

Loch Ness is famous the world over for its legendary monster. Many sightings have been claimed and a certain amount of questionable photographic evidence obtained, but there has yet to be any indisputable proof.

To that end, a Scottish university research project was launched in 1986 to try and discover any remains, given that sightings of the monster stretch back for several hundred years. If the creatures exist they would have a limited lifespan, so there should be skeletons on the loch floor.

The search duly began and seemed to be on to something when the underwater video camera displayed a long cage-like structure, partially covered with strands of a thin outer lining. Hopes that this was perhaps the decaying ribcage of a recently deceased creature were dashed when it was realised that the structure was in fact the remains of an old aircraft.

However this in itself became a major discovery when the aircraft was identified as 'R for Robert', a World War Two Wellington Bomber that had ditched into the loch on a training flight in 1940. While unremarkable at the time, it was now the only 'surviving' craft of its type that had seen active service, all other wartime Wellingtons having been broken down for scrap after the war.

So a salvage attempt was launched to lift the plane from its muddy forty-year grave, restore it to its former glory and display it with full honours in the RAF museum.

The salvage caught the attention of the national media, because of the loch's legend and the faint hope that Nessie might make a guest appearance. The local hoteliers, not ones to miss out on a veritable stampede of gift horses, immediately doubled their rates on the assumption that everyone was going to be on lavish expenses and therefore unlikely to complain. Obviously they've never worked for the BBC.

A BBC documentary team had begun filming the salvage operation but needed a relief crew, so I travelled up to

Scotland with Andy (cameraman) and Mike (sound recordist) to join the media circus.

Our filming had an inauspicious start. We set off onto the loch in the middle of what the locals described as 'a bit of a blow'. I'd always imagined Scottish lochs to be havens of peace and tranquillity, with only the gentle lapping of the ripples to disturb one's quest for a giant salmon. So much for the tourist spiel. The setting was more like Sink The Bismark than Raise The Wellington. Waves crashed over our small hired pleasure cruiser and by lunchtime we had suffered two casualties: the delicate inner workings of our camera and the even more delicate inner workings of our land-loving sound recordist, who spent most of the morning below deck pleading for a swift and merciful death.

Our 'pleasure' cruiser lurched back to the quayside and we retired to our rooms at McRipoffs to dry out and recuperate. As Andy worked on repairing the camera and Mike gradually became distinguishable from the green wallpaper I remarked to Alex, the production assistant, that we hadn't exactly got off to a good start.

'Oh, things could have been worse,' she replied. 'Last week our boat sprang a leak.' I made a note to check out the life-jackets.

We recommenced filming the next day and were grateful to reach the stability of the large barge that served as a diving platform directly above the crash site some two hundred feet down. Having heard tales of luxury conditions on North Sea oil rigs, I was surprised at the compete lack of anything on the platform, except large pools of oil, piles of heavy machinery and a Spartan control room, where a simple plastic chair would have elevated the decor to levels undreamed of at Versailles. The charm of the place soon began to wear thin.

The control room boasted a couple of video monitors, which relayed the progress of the divers. The plan was to attach the Wellington to a specially designed lifting cradle, but unfortunately the plane was tangled in a large trawling net that had to be cleared away first. As trawling was not exactly common in the loch, the net was probably the result of some hair-brained past attempt to catch Nessie.

Another problem for the divers was the suits they had to wear. Working at a depth of two hundred feet for long periods made conventional scuba techniques inappropriate, and so the divers were encased in robot-like steel diving suits with hydraulic arms. These were so large that they (and the diver inside) had to be winched off and on the platform by crane. To Nessie they must have seemed like canned meat.

The following evening the lifting cradle for the Wellington was launched and hours of lethargy gave way to a few mad minutes of dashing around and jostling with other television crews. However as soon as the cradle disappeared below the waves, we were back to more shots of murky video monitors, general views around the platform and the occasional comment from the salvage team leader. He'd perfected dour sullenness to an art form, so every enquiry elicited the same terse response: 'We won't know anything until we try and lift her.' Thank you and good night.

The next day we hung around the platform waiting for developments. The prospect for the day after seemed even bleaker as the weather forecast predicted a storm, making any work impossible. The divers greeted this news with relief and after several long cold days under water they relaxed that night in the hotel with a spectacular display of alcohol abuse. Unfortunately the forecast was wrong and early next morning they were back on duty, but now very much the worse for wear. One diver was in particularly bad shape, and fearing a reaction to the previous night's excesses, took a bin liner down with him. That's dedication for you.

As on the previous days there was little worth filming. It became clear that the salvage was much more complex than expected and as money for the attempt was running low, it was beginning to look as if the Wellington might be staying put for another forty years.

Deadlines came and went, each being postponed because of some technical hitch or the weather. Mike Smart, the reporter for BBC News was struggling for something new to say in his reports.

'I've already used "time is running out/hopes are fading fast/a last ditch effort/it's do or die/all or nothing on this final attempt/positively the last chance/a last gasp effort/it's salvage or bust/it's now or never/a last minute reprieve/the weather has closed in as we approach the final deadline/grim and strained faces among the salvage crew tell their own story" - I've run out of clichés.'

'Have you mentioned the lovely scenery?' we suggested helpfully.

The TV crews spent their days hanging around in the cold and wet of the diving platform but the gentlemen of the press, as nothing of any consequence was actually happening, were able to relax in their customary manner at the hotel bar. All of the major dailies were there, including of course the Sun. Their reporter's grasp of events was perfectly displayed one night after everyone had spent five days talking about the Wellington, how it was the last surviving Wellington, how it was being salvaged by the Wellington Preservation Society, and so on:

'So, when do you think they're going to lift the Lancaster?'

By Day Seven the salvage team was finally ready to lift the plane from the loch floor. The media mob assembled on the platform, hoping to see the Wellington rise from the waves. The long hours of waiting were forgotten amid the tension and anticipation. The winches took the strain and began to haul up the cradle. Suddenly there was a screeching sound and the cables went limp. Something had obviously gone wrong. A report came through from below. The cradle had collapsed under the strain.

The salvage attempt was over.

Some time later we filmed the crumpled wreckage of the cradle as it broke the surface of the loch and was dumped on the platform. The post-mortem revealed that while the cradle's fifteen-ton lifting capacity was more than adequate for the eleven-ton plane, what had not been anticipated was the suction effect of the heavy mud in and around the plane, which virtually doubled its weight.

With the rescue attempt apparently over, the media packed up and headed south. While I was personally disappointed that the attempt had failed, my sympathies lay largely with the divers. During the week we had got to know them well and I was sorry that their countless hours in the cold and darkness had come to naught.

On arriving back at base in Yorkshire we heard that the BBC had been trying to contact us with instructions to return immediately to the loch. Apparently the salvage company had decided to go for broke and built a simple lifting cradle consisting of two steel girders welded together. This was lowered into the water, the plane attached to it and then simply hauled up. Easy. So much for the specially designed lifting cradle.

Unfortunately by the time we received the message (this was BM - Before Mobiles), the BBC had contacted another crew who probably passed us on their way north as we headed south. So after a cold and wet week hanging around on the diving platform we missed the story, and I had to wait for the documentary to see the Wellington's return from the loch.

Nevertheless the week was not all loss. I had witnessed the incredible thirst of journalists and industrial divers for expenses-paid alcohol (no surprises there). I had seen a top news reporter scrape his barrel of clichés (ditto). And I had discovered that to those in the know, the Wellington has a particular nick-name. I was standing outside the hotel when I was approached by a man in his sixties.

'Where's the Wimpey?' he asked.

'Oh, I think there's one in the town but I'm not sure if they're open on Sundays.'

I received what I can only describe as one of those 'I-fought-in-the-War-for-cheeky-young-buggers-like-you' looks.

The years of living dangerously

A film came out a few years ago entitled *Risky Business* starring some young unknown called Tom Cruise (who?) I've always felt that the title describes the business of film-making itself: the financial risks taken by the producers, who can make fortunes or end up bankrupt; the artistic risks taken by the actors, who striving for a performance that veers away from the safe and conventional, can end up being ridiculed by the critics. And then there are the physical risks involved in actually making the film.

The most obvious physical risks are during the filming of stunts, but these generally pass without incident because everyone is aware of the dangers and takes the necessary safety precautions. Imminent peril does wonders for the concentration. It's difficult to be blasé when you're perched on a cliff edge, standing uncomfortably close to an explosion or lying next to the path of an approaching car. There are occasions, however, when even with meticulous planning, it can still all go wrong.

I was working at Elstree film studios on a documentary about the making of the third Indiana Jones film, *The Last Crusade*, starring Harrison Ford and Sean Connery. The scene for that day was set in the castle where Indy and his father (played by Connery) had been captured by the Germans and were now securely bound to a couple of chairs. In attempting to break free Indy knocks over a candle and starts a fire. To escape the flames the two heroes shuffle over to the fireplace, where Indy accidentally hits a hidden switch and the fireplace revolves, taking them away from the flames but into a room full of Germans (out of the fire into the frying pan). That, anyway, was the plan.

The set was ringed by professional firefighters whose job (perversely) was to set fire to the furniture and drapes, and then be ready to dash in and douse the flames as soon as Spielberg yelled, 'Cut!' Three cameras were positioned on the edge of the set well away from the flames. The set was then ignited, the cameras started rolling and the two stars began struggling to break free of their bonds.

The scene seemed to be going on rather long, when above the roar of the flames Connery and Ford could be heard yelling, 'Turn, turn!' But the fireplace stayed where it was. Obviously something had gone wrong and two of Hollywood's hottest were getting hotter by the second. Spielberg immediately stopped shooting and the flames were doused, in true Indy tradition, in the nick of time.

In the post-mortem it transpired that the two crew operating the fireplace revolve had not heard their cue, and being unable to see the action had not appreciated how serious the situation was becoming. The communication problem was sorted out and a second take was set up, but Connery refused to take part. He has the reputation of being the consummate professional and expects the same of those around him. This little hiccup had not gone down well with him. 'If they can't get it right first time then get the doubles to do it', he said and walked off the set. Which in the end is what happened.

So, even the best laid plans by the cream of technical talent can go awry.

Covering the news can present the highest risks, from the obvious dangers of Bosnia and Belfast to sudden attacks from angry crowds or aggrieved individuals who don't take kindly to being featured on the evening bulletin.

The hazard factor can also be high in documentaries. Sure, some of the environments are dangerous - oil rigs, mines, building sites, shipyards - but probably the major cause of accidents is the working attitude that can develop. Adrenalin, fatigue, excitement, pressure of deadlines, the desire to get a difficult shot, all can undermine both one's natural instincts for self-preservation and any 'sensible' precautions that may have been taken. When this occurs even an 'everyday' situation can become hazardous, e.g. stepping back off a pavement to get a wider shot of a building. I've been guilty myself of such lapses but nowadays, after a few scrapes and a couple of too-close calls I'm hopefully a little wiser.

A few months ago I was discussing an upcoming documentary with the producer and at one point he said, 'You're a gung-ho sort of chap, aren't you?' There was a time when my reaction would have been 'Yea, sure, bring on the hang-gliders', but now the remark set alarm bells jangling. When the gung-ho situation arrives it's rare to find such producers in the thick of things - they are usually on the sidelines on a cellphone exhorting more gung-ho. (One notable exception was a trip to a remote island to film a live volcano. With a thunderstorm approaching, we were about to board an alarmingly small helicopter for a thirty-minute journey over rough seas. As I stored away the last piece of equipment the producer, who was coming with us, rushed up to me and said, 'Would you mind witnessing my new will?' That's when you *know* you're in trouble.)

The Lloyds Insurance building in central London was constructed to a chorus of bouquets and brickbats, winning awards for architectural design while simultaneously invoking criticism for its 'boiler factory' array of pipes and tubes. One particular feature was the high-speed clear-glass lifts on the outside corners of the building, offering spectacular and vertiginous views of London as one sped between floors.

The director wanted a shot that started in darkness and then moved upwards to reveal the City of London in all its glory. The lifts at Lloyds provided the perfect 'crane' and so we negotiated exclusive use of one for a couple of hours. The camera was set up inside the lift but the shot was being spoiled by some dirt on the outside of the glass. Cleaning the glass presented a problem because there was no external ground-level access to the lift, as it went straight from the enclosed basement to our present position some fifteen feet above street level. However some construction work was being carried out and the hoarding round the site provided access of sorts to the outside of the lift.

I'm still not quite sure why, but I volunteered to climb along the top of the hoarding and tackle the glass from the outside. We arranged for one of the Lloyds staff to keep the 'Doors Open' button pressed to stop the lift being called to another floor, and I edged my way cautiously along the one-inch edge of the hoarding, leaning against the lift for support. I finally reached the problem area and began to clean away the offending marks.

I never actually heard a countdown but the lift suddenly took off like a Shuttle launch and I was left perched precariously on top of the hoarding.

I can't say my life flashed before my eyes, but in the sudden rush of adrenalin I knew that I was in an extremely serious (if somewhat ludicrous) situation. To my left was a drop of about fifteen feet to the pavement below. If I was lucky I might get away with a broken leg. To my right were the yawning depths of the lift shaft with the basement somewhere below in the darkness. If I went over that way, luck wouldn't get a look-in.

I decided to stay where I was. I assumed the lift would return.

As the seconds dragged by, my legs began to shake and I felt my balance beginning to go. I considered jumping off in the hope of grabbing hold of the hoarding but decided to leave this as a drastic final option.

Help then came from an unexpected quarter.

Along the pavement beneath me came a couple of London City's Hooray Henrys. They had seen the lift's dramatic departure and were observing my predicament with sadistic delight.

'Oh look, Nigel, they're making a m-o-o-vie!'

'OK yar Spielberg way to go.'

(There's never an Uzi handy when you need one.)

I was damned if I was going to give them the satisfaction of seeing me fall off. New-found energy came to my legs as I grimly concentrated on staying upright.

Eventually I heard the whirr of the returning lift. If nothing else, I was determined to come out of the affair with a certain kudos. As the lift settled back into place I simply ignored the occupants and carried on cleaning the glass as if nothing had happened.

When I worked my way back off the hoarding I heard the other half of the story. Although the Lloyds staff member had kept her finger religiously pressed on the 'Doors Open' button, she was unaware that this could be over-ridden by a call from the top floor - which housed the offices of the Managing Director.

So the lift took off, leaving me in my Keatonesque dilemma - to which the instant reaction from the crew inside the lift was a collapse into uncontrollable laughter. Bastards.

On arrival at the top floor the Managing Director of Lloyds Insurance was met by an hysterical bunch of film technicians, all doubled up with laughter and yelling at him, 'You can't come in! You can't come in!' At which point the doors closed and the lift disappeared, leaving the most powerful person in Lloyds standing.

On reflection, I'm glad I didn't follow my initial plan to tackle the glass by climbing on top of the lift.

Covering the attempt to lift the Wellington Bomber from Loch Ness was a largely uneventful week as far as the story was concerned, but it did involve boats, which always hold great potential for injury. Over the seven days I managed to rack up a few incidents from the minor to the near fatal.

On the first day I slipped as I was climbing aboard our boat, crashing heavily into the side of the craft and bruising a couple of ribs. Great start.

Three days later we were trying to transfer from our small boat to the diving barge in the middle of the loch. The wind had whipped up the waves, making the transfer a risky affair, as one second the two craft would be level with each other and the next our small vessel would drop down five feet. Timing, as they say, was everything.

We managed to get the gear safely across, but as I tried to clamber aboard the barge our boat suddenly dropped away, leaving me hanging from the side of the barge. The next second the boat rose up and crashed heavily into the side of the barge just three feet to my left. I didn't hang around to observe the next point of contact and managed to scramble aboard the barge and collapse on deck.

Not that I was the only person to have a few scrapes. During one of the boat-to-boat transfers one of the news sound recordists was awaiting his turn to make the jump. His hand was resting on the handrail when the rope connecting the two craft suddenly went taut, snapping down on to the rail and neatly breaking one of his fingers.

'Oh, I've just broken my finger,' he announced, matter-of-factly. Ten minutes later the shock had set in, dismissing any further display of bravado.

'Lucky not to lose his hand,' remarked one of the divers.

As the week progressed we grew accustomed to being on call at night. The rescue attempt had become more desperate and the divers were taking whatever opportunity they could to advance the salvage. One particular evening we were filming a flurry of activity in the central deck area, now flooded with light from the powerful overhead working lamps. The cameraman wanted another lens urgently, so I turned towards our equipment cases on the dark side of the deck.

Wham.

I still don't know what Arnie Schwarzenegger was doing on-board that night, nor why he decided to hit me in the face with a ten-pound hammer. At least that's what it felt like. My night vision ruined by the working lights, I had run full pelt into an iron spar positioned conveniently at eye height. The blow knocked me backwards on to the deck.

'You OK?' asked a concerned voice.

'Yea, fine, thanks,' I mumbled, blood pouring down the side of my face. Funny thing, pride. I was too embarrassed at my stupidity to admit to the pain throbbing through my head. When I later examined the damage I saw that the spar had caught my left eye on the edge of the socket. Half an inch to the right and I would have been blinded.

After a catalogue of near misses it was perhaps inevitable
that I would eventually sustain some sort of serious injury.
We were filming in Rotterdam container port, an inherently
dangerous place to be. Large container carriers, four storeys
high and oddly reminiscent of the alien machines in *The War
of the Worlds*, raced about at great speed, apparently
unaware of what was going on at ground level. Accidents
had happened in the past, with a couple of the carriers
toppling over while cornering too quickly. Recently a
ground-level worker had been crushed when a container had
been lowered on top of him.

We set up the camera on the tripod to film one of the
carriers speeding down a line of containers. As soon as we
had the ground-level shot, we were to run up a nearby tower
for a high-angle shot of the same scene before the machine
disappeared from view. With the first shot completed, I
picked up the heavy tripod, slung it over my shoulder and
ran towards the staircase. As I ran up the first flight the
tripod slipped back and over-balanced, pulling my left arm
back violently. I felt a sickening crunch and agonizing pain
as it dislocated my shoulder.

Being a natural coward and not a bit like Mel Gibson (no,
really) I was not up to the usual movie machismo of
personally yanking my shoulder back into place before
giving the villains a well-deserved thrashing. Instead I chose
to wait forty minutes with a Valium injection that relaxed
the muscles and eventually allowed the joint to be eased
back into place.

More haste, less speed.

When Leonardo da Vinci outlined his design for the
helicopter some five hundred years ago he probably didn't
realise its potential use for the film industry. Just goes to
show that even a genius has his off-days.

Nevertheless the helicopter has become a standard
filming platform and most cameramen have experienced the
delights of a flight with the side door removed: the cold, the

noise, the air sickness, the stomach-churning turns - you can't beat it.

Unfortunately through a series of accidents over the years, the helicopter has acquired a reputation for being perhaps not the safest means of exposing film stock. But it's still an exciting craft and the buzz of that first flight far outweighs any first-time nerves. So if you get the chance, go for a ride and save the nerves for later trips. Assuming you survive your first, that is - which I nearly didn't.

It was wintertime, freezing and we were flying over the smoke stacks and furnaces of industrial Teesside. Like I keep telling people, I'm only in this job for the chicks, the glamour and the fast cars.

We had been up in the air about ten minutes and I was sitting in the rear left-hand passenger seat noting down shot details (part of the camera assistant's job) when the pilot suddenly executed a steep banking turn to the left. The door next to me swung open, leaving me peering straight down to the earth some five hundred feet below. I was saved from an abrupt exit only by my seat belt. When we levelled up I managed to slam the door shut, at which point the pilot swung around with a look of alarm, obviously thinking that one of his passengers had just stepped outside for a breath of fresh air.

On returning to base the door catch was found to be faulty. Profuse apologies were offered, but I was silently giving thanks for all those subconsciously conditioning safety films that the Beeb used to show before close-down. Clunk click every trip.

Probably nowhere in the world is the steam train more avidly worshipped than in Britain. Despite being dealt a virtual death blow by the switch to diesel during the 1960s, the preservation societies and Those Who Shall Wear Anoraks have saved many of the great beasts of smoke and steam from the scrap heap.

As part of the BBC series *Steam Days* we were filming Sir Nigel Gressley (the engine, not the person) shunting back and forth at the Carnforth Railway Museum in Lancashire. Carnforth Station is best known for having been the location for Sir David Lean's film *Brief Encounter*, that wonderful study of English middle-class passion being kept firmly in check by stiff upper lips and extraordinary vowel sounds. The setting proved to be rather apt as I had my own brief encounter with Sir Nigel.

Only when you get up close to a steam engine do you begin to appreciate its size and power. (It was made very clear to me by Those Who Know that one refers to a steam engine rather than a steam train, as a train comprises an engine, tender, carriages, the whole kit and caboodle.) We had spent the morning filming Sir Nigel as it (he?) was put through its paces and I was getting rather blasé about scuttling around the enormous wheels as we went in for close-ups.

We were doing a simple 'up-and-past' shot with Sir Nigel looming large in frame. The engine and tender went past at a reasonable lick and I started to walk across the tracks for the next shot, my attention centred on completing my notes for the preceding scene.

I think it's usually referred to as sixth sense, but something made me look up to see Sir Nigel, having made a manoeuvre akin to a handbrake turn, now reversing towards me at an alarming rate. The driver was unable to see me because I was actually walking between the rails. I dived forward, expecting any second to have my legs dragged under the wheels of the tender. It was, as Wellington said, a damn close run thing.

Moral of the tale? Don't walk into the path of several tons of heavy machinery travelling at a rate of knots.

Particularly if it's called Nigel.

The joys of travel

One of the big pluses of working in television is the chance
for foreign travel. It's just one big expenses-paid holiday
with a few snaps thrown in for good measure. Well anyway,
that's the popular myth that I'd now like to try and dispel.
Fat chance, but here goes.

Despite the glamorous image, the reality is less to do
with lounging around the hotel swimming pool waiting for
the right light and more to do with endless travel, complete
with about ten times as much luggage as your average
holiday-maker. The long working days squeeze in as much
filming as possible while the crew attempt to survive the
vagaries of the local cuisine, traffic and sometimes politics
in order to stay well enough to complete the job. I've yet to
meet a producer who says, 'I'd like you to work on this job
abroad. It's going to be really easy and there'll be lots of
time off. In fact it'll be more like a holiday.'

Before you can take equipment overseas you have to
compile a minutely detailed list for a customs document
called a carnet. This allows equipment to enter and leave a
foreign country without being examined or incurring duty -
much to the chagrin of customs, who seem to believe that
you've simply come to flog the gear tax-free in the nearest
bar. Every piece of equipment has to be listed, along with its
reference number, value and country of origin, and each
carrying case specified by size and weight. All in triplicate,
with two sets of documents for each country visited. And I
thought I'd found a job that didn't involve paperwork.

So you turn up early for your flight and check in the gear.
This takes about an hour and annoys the hell out of the
people behind you in the queue. And as it slips down the
luggage belt you utter a silent prayer that approximately the
same number of pieces will arrive at the other end. That, of
course, depends on those doyens of delicate dispatch, the
baggage handlers.

Before I completely alienate a section of possible readership I have to say that the major airlines usually treat film equipment well. It is only once you venture into uncharted airspace that problems begin to occur. Despite plastering all the cases with 'Fragile' labels, I still remember seeing a case of lenses being tossed from the luggage hold of a 747, missed by the intended catcher and dropping on the tarmac. I looked at the cameraman. I've never seen a face move so rapidly from healthy tan to sickly white. It was only thanks to the high-tech construction and padding of the case that the lenses survived.

Once you arrive at your destination you face the local customs. If you've ever been hauled over the coals by customs for a single suitcase, imagine the fun and games trying to get thirty cases of film gear past them. I'm sure that during training, customs officers are indoctrinated to believe that film crews are the embodiment of evil and as such must be cast from this earth.

'Major drug trafficker, sir? Right, thank you very much and enjoy your stay. Next....oh, so you're part of a film crew are you, sir? Step to one side, please, and open these cases - every one of them.'

In a perfect world you should be spared such humiliation by producing a carnet, but if a customs officer wants you to make his day, all you can do is bite your tongue and be extra polite, or you could be hanging around the airport for hours. On one occasion a Japanese customs officer queried a filter case which contained sixty-nine filters whereas the carnet stated only sixty-six. The cameraman resolved the problem by removing three and putting them in his pocket. Customs and carnet were now satisfied.

Working overseas in a hot climate usually elicits envy and yes, sailing around the Greek islands does beat working in a London studio. But such locations also create problems. You need a fridge to keep the film stock cool and a hundred cans of film won't fit in the hotel mini-bar (assuming there's a hotel and assuming there's a mini-bar). Getting extra equipment or stock from home is also fraught with difficulties. Transit time, weekends, public holidays, religious festivals and strikes by absolutely anybody can all conspire to ensure that your vital supplies arrive in Athens three days after you've set sail for Turkey.

That apart, religion and politics are two safe bets for causing hassles. Any trip to a Muslim country provides endless opportunities for unintentional offence, and the simplest misunderstanding can flare up into a major incident. The security situation in the Middle East is so sensitive that anybody with a camera is immediately under suspicion. Always in the back of your mind there's the fear that the film and equipment could be confiscated and you and your colleagues arrested on spying charges - or worse, taken hostage.

Being an English-speaking crew attracts a lot of attention when filming out on the streets. Most of it is just good-natured curiosity, but occasionally you come up against someone who, for whatever reason, takes great offence to you being there. It doesn't take much for a misunderstanding to get out of hand. Then the shouting starts, the police arrive and it all ends up in a trip down to the local station to try and sort things out. You may not speak the language but diplomatic smiles and open body language are invaluable for defusing the situation.

Assuming you've managed to film something without being hassled, threatened or arrested, there is the problem of getting the 'rushes' (the exposed film) safely back to the processing lab in England. Airfreighting from, say, Egypt or Turkey, a large sealed carton that has to be handled gently, kept away from heat and not subjected to physical examination or X-rays can present the occasional tiny problem.

Then there's the rushes report from the lab. Lab technicians can vary in their opinions on rushes and it's easy to give the wrong impression. A vague reference to a blemish on the footage can create havoc when reported to a crew several thousand miles away. The camera crew peer hopefully into the back of the camera while the production team hurriedly schedule a reshoot for the affected scene. On eventual viewing, however, the flaw may be minimal and acceptable, or covered by another shot, and a lot of time and nervous energy has been expended for nothing.

So there you have it, an inside view of what filming abroad is really like. Now do you believe that it's not just a cruisy holiday?

No, I didn't think so.

No, we're not the BBC

'How about "No, I don't know anyone famous"?'

Mike (cameraman) and I were going to Spain for a five-week shoot and were discussing a motto for a sun hat that I wanted to buy. I knew enough about sun protection to realise that I needed some sort of a hat, but I wanted something a bit different. A hat that made a statement. A hat to launch a thousand quips.

I had several ideas, all replies to questions that film crews are forever asked by the public. Mike thought for a second and then came up with the clincher.

'What about "No, we're not the BBC"?'

It clicked instantly. Any British film crew anywhere in the world is automatically assumed to be from the BBC, and on this particular occasion the words would be perfect as we were going to be working for Channel 4 - although I was later to rue denying the influence which the Beeb carries worldwide.

The trip to Spain was part of an enormous project entitled *The Encircled Sea* about the history of the Mediterranean and its surrounding countries. The series consisted of ten half-hour programmes, each devoted to a particular theme - warfare, trade, fishing, navigation and so on. The filming was going to take the best part of a year, with separate trips to each country lasting anything from two to six weeks. As a professional project it was quite daunting and by far the biggest job I'd ever done.

We began in Malaga, birthplace of Picasso and 'capital' of the Costa del Sol, the stretch of holiday resorts that runs along the south coast of Spain from Malaga down to Gibralter. After successfully negotiating customs with our mountain of equipment, we met the Spanish contingent who were to be our local contacts and drivers.

The most senior Spaniard was the production manager, Federico, on loan from Spanish Television, who were one of

the financial backers. With an open, boyish face and ready
smile he was instantly likeable, and I was relieved that we
did not appear destined for the kind of professional rivalry
that often mars relations with foreign crews. I did, however,
fail to notice the manic twinkle in the eyes. Only as the
weeks progressed and events became more hectic did his
true personality emerge.

Assisting Federico were two drivers, Leo and Victor. Leo
was short, slim and wiry, probably in his thirties, but the
effects of the sun on his weather-beaten face made it
difficult to judge his age. He spoke no English at all and his
Spanish came either in rapid machine-gun bursts or, if you
obviously didn't understand, he would repeat the sentence,
as the English do when abroad, slowly and very loudly. If
you were still none the wiser, he would turn to Federico with
a gesture of 'How can anyone be so stupid?' and get him to
translate. Nevertheless it was all done without malice and we
were to have many animated and enjoyable conversations
with neither party having the foggiest idea what the other
was saying.

Victor was much younger, about eighteen, with the kind
of swarthy good looks and laid-back sleepy manner that
reminded me of the waiters who used to nick my girlfriends
during early holidays to Spain. Victor didn't speak any
English but seemed to understand the occasional word,
which was useful when I wanted to practise my appalling
Spanish.

Our first day in Malaga was spent filming the Alcazaba,
the magnificent Moorish castle, and the cathedral, La
Manquita ('the one-armed woman'), so-named because only
one of the two towers was ever completed. The idea was to
illustrate Muslim influence up to the fifteenth century when
the Moors were expelled by the Christians, and then
compare this influence with the modern-day return of Arabs
to the area via vast property developments.

Hence Marbella, one of the more expensive resorts on the
coast, boasted an Arab bank and an Arab-owned apartment
complex with units priced at over £1,000,000 each. Further

along the coast there were several new mosques, including one for the exclusive use of the King of Saudi Arabia, whose private residence was a scaled-down replica of the White House in Washington. If you can't beat 'em....

Somebody somewhere must have pulled a few strings for us, as we seemed to be getting some pretty high-profile attention. Two motorcycle police would guard our van while we were away filming and as we drove through the streets of Malaga our outriders would speed ahead to clear a path through the traffic. I began practising a presidential wave. This was style. I could get used to this. Unfortunately the preferential treatment disappeared after the first day, but it was nice while it lasted.

As the week progressed we worked our way along the Costa del Sol. This involved driving along N340, the notorious Highway of Death that runs along the southern coast. It is officially designated as *peligrossimo*, highly dangerous. The locals call it 'the four-lane mortuary'.

We arrived in Torremolinos, which had obviously decided to become Southend. The cafes boasted egg'n'chips, fish'n'chips, Typhoo Tea or Bisto gravy, all designed to save the English tourist from 'that greasy foreign food'. The tower-block hotels had been built so close to the sands that by mid-afternoon the beach was largely in shadow, forcing the hordes of pink flesh to cram into an ever-decreasing strip between the encroaching tide and the dreaded sun-block.

In Puerto Banus, the 'retirement resort' for some of London's more successful villains, we spied a few likely lads, complete with accessory blondes. On seeing our camera one or two beat a hasty retreat. I heard a few combinations of pidgin Spanish and Cockney rhyming slang that were surprisingly absent from my holiday phrase book.

''Ere Pedro, donde esta el jam jar?'

By the end of the first week we had bonded into a pretty efficient unit. We were also getting to know our Spanish contingent better. With our production team constantly changing the schedule, Federico's natural exuberance was becoming frenetic, and his initially excellent English gave way to an impassioned form of Spanglish. George, our sound recordist, consulted his English-Spanish dictionary in an attempt to pass on a few words of comfort, although I don't think, 'Federico, don't get your bragas in a torsa' actually helped a great deal.

Leo was great fun, but drove the same way that he spoke Spanish, at high speed and with little regard for anyone else. He would drive the lead car containing Federico, Geoff (the director) and Julia (the production assistant), while Victor followed in the camera van with myself, Mike and George. Every journey was accompanied by much jabbering of directions over walkie-talkies. Leo would always streak off into the distance, leaving Federico to give instructions to Victor, who was by then several hundred yards behind.

Making a simple left turn became a major navigational exercise.

'We are coming up to a left turn by the church on the left-hand side. You will see it on the left, next to the church. We are about to turn left any moment now. Can you see us? We are turning left, turning left....'

(*Sound of screeching tyres accompanied by a variety of oaths in Spanish and English.*)

'We have turned left, turned left, can you see where we turned? On the left-hand side, by the church, on the left.'

After a particularly close encounter with a truck, Geoff called both vehicles over to the roadside, and shaking with rage conveyed to both Leo and Victor the principles of convoy driving. Given their lack of English, Geoff's explanation had to be accompanied by pantomime gestures, but an understanding seem to be reached when Leo and Victor finally nodded in agreement. Then they returned to the cars and carried on as before.

While Leo's driving may have been fast, he was otherwise a reliable member of the crew. Victor however was becoming a bit of a worry. His driving was scary and there were always a few adrenalin-boosting incidents to keep us buzzing.

Moreover he was always turning up late, hung over, unshaven and stinking to high heaven in the previous day's clothes. We discovered that he was carousing till dawn in the local clubs, so that he would arrive in the morning knackered from another night's amorous conquest and in no fit state to drive us. Mike and I had requisitioned the rear seats, so George was left in the front to cope with the dual menace of Victor's driving and personal hygiene. At times the latter would be so overpowering that George would spend entire journeys with his head stuck out of the window like the crew pet Labrador.

It was clear that Victor would have to go and so, after several warnings and ultimatums, he was finally sacked. Strangely he seemed genuinely unaware what the problem was and left me a rather touching note in broken English asking me to write and explain what had happened. To my shame I never got around to replying, but when this book goes into worldwide sales, I hope he will read it and understand.

Victor's replacement was a middle-aged man called Alfonso, solid in both stature and personality. His only words of English were 'No problem' and his steady driving and general all-round ability tackling any task soon earned him the nickname of 'No-Problem-Alfonso'. At the end of each day we would voice our gratitude for his safe driving and assistance with a crew chorus of 'Viva Alfonso!', to which we received the inevitable response.

We eventually left the tourist strip of the coast and moved west to Tarifa, a small fishing town on the southernmost tip of Spain, so-called because of its original role as a tariff collection point for ships passing into the Med.

We were there to film the impressive Roman ruins, which consisted of large stone pits that had originally been built for storing locally-caught tuna destined for Rome. The area was fenced off for security reasons, but we were allowed to roam as we pleased and I spent the afternoon happily clambering in and out of the eight-foot deep pits. At the end of the day we packed up the gear and returned to the van. I asked our local guide why she had stayed outside the fence all afternoon rather than join us among the ruins.

'Too many snakes.'

Two thousand years on from the Romans, tuna were still being caught, but by a unique method. Instead of the usual trawling, the fishermen would spend several days building a maze of nets. Having entered the maze, the tuna would keep swimming until they arrived at the centre, the 'chamber of death'. Here these magnificent 600-plus pound creatures would meet their fate in a bloody orgy of killing, a scene I was grateful we were not going to be covering.

We went out on a fishing boat to where the nets were being laid, but to get in among the fishermen we had to clamber aboard a small rowing boat. Filming from the tiny craft in a choppy sea was not easy, but the images were superb and the scenes timeless: old men with grizzled faces, sinewy arms and skin like leather - plus an admirable savvy of modern filming techniques. Whenever we stopped to reposition, change magazines or put on a clapperboard, everybody would pause, wait until we were ready and then continue with their activities, ensuring that their best side was always to camera. They'd probably done more docos than we had.

We wanted to illustrate the flow of illegal drugs into Spain, mostly from nearby Morocco. To this end we arranged to film the coastguard in action, but as it wasn't feasible to accompany them on an actual 'bust', we had to construct our own scenario.

The plan seemed quite straightforward. We would go up in a helicopter and take general shots of the coastguard launch as it powered through the water. Then we'd land, board the boat and repeat the sequence, taking close-ups of the crew. However we hadn't allowed for Spanish pride and the serious consequences if you offended it.

The word had obviously got around coastguard headquarters that we were here to film them in action. As a result, we turned up at the location after lunch to find not the standard complement of a captain and five crew, but three captains and fifteen crew, all immaculately turned out and eager for stardom. Just how eager they were became apparent when we explained how we wanted to approach the sequence.

The crew insisted that we had to film from the launch first before going up in the helicopter, because they were concerned that once we had obtained our aerial shots we wouldn't be interested in filming their close-ups on the boat. Geoff assured the captains that we needed both viewpoints for the sequence, but that we wouldn't know what shots we wanted from the boat until we had seen them in action from the air.

The captains dug in their heels and persisted with their demand, which was translated by an increasingly agitated Federico as the discussion became more heated. These negotiations continued well into the afternoon until eventually Geoff issued an ultimatum that unless he, the director, was allowed to direct the sequence as he saw fit, the filming would be cancelled. The threat of not appearing on television at all won the day and after a short discussion the three captains agreed to accede to Geoff's wishes.

We climbed into the helicopter and prepared to start filming. It was now six o'clock in the evening and we hadn't shot a frame of film all day.

Filming from helicopters is commonplace and I've been on more trips than I care to remember, plus a few that I would definitely prefer to forget. The key factor in the success or otherwise of filming from the air is the pilot, who determines the height and position of the camera, the angle and speed of approach, and so on.

Because of the incredible manoeuvrability of the craft, a pilot can make a helicopter do almost anything, sometimes with stomach-churning results. For the first couple of trips it's a buzz, but after a while you begin to appreciate the pilot who will simply take you up, get the shots required with the minimum fuss and then gently and safely bring you back to earth. The kind of guy for whom safety is the prime objective. The kind of guy who keeps the aerobatics to a minimum. The kind of guy we did not have as our pilot on this trip.

Called Alfonso (not to be confused with our driver), he was definitely one of life's characters. Of indeterminate age due to his grizzled appearance, we discovered that he spent six months of the year crop-spraying in Texas, to which his peaked baseball cap bore witness with the legend 'Tap Worm Killer'. His favourite expression was 'Son of a gun!' and this affection for the Wild West seemed to influence his flying. The passes over the coastguard launch became lower and lower and the turns ever tighter. After one particularly close encounter he shouted over the intercom, 'Son of a gun Mike, that was a close one!' I just shut my eyes and thought of England.

As no drug smugglers were kind enough to turn up for the filming, the coastguard decided to do a dummy check on a passing fishing boat - except that no one bothered to inform the fishermen. As the shooting began it became obvious that our Spanish law enforcers had been watching too many episodes of *Miami Vice*.

The crew on the trawler never knew what hit them.

First Two-Gun Tex buzzed them at a level that would have had the tap worms in Texas shakin' in their boots. Then one of the coastguard's powerboats screamed across their bows. Finally the launch brought up the rear, ensuring no chance of escape for these international traffickers and their immoral haul of sardines, gambas and flatfish.

The aerial scenes over, we returned to port and were immediately rushed into the powerboat. It almost left the water as we headed out to the main launch, all of fifty yards away. We could have rowed out, but the boys wanted to show off the toys. Out at the launch, willing hands hauled us on-board and the powerful engines creamed up the bay as we chased, well, nothing. But hey, the audience don't know that and image is everything.

On deck our cast were still playing out their roles of Crocket and Tubbs, the *Miami Vice* theme no doubt pounding in their brains as they mouthed Spanish versions of 'Freeze, scumball, or you're history.'

We filmed the Captain as he struggled with his powerful craft and equally powerful urge to grin maniacally at the camera. The waves crashed over the bow, Alfonso screamed low overhead and the powerboat crew did their best to ensure their share of screen time by making dramatic passes in the near background. The Captain and his two associates at the wheel were being lashed by spray but never once did they shirk their quest for the best position to camera.

Finally we called it a day and everybody relaxed as we headed back to port. It had been a furious few hours and my middle ear had been pounded like never before. Suffering from a combination of air and sea sickness, I went below decks so that I could concentrate on being really ill.

The Mediterranean has the reputation of being one of the most polluted seas on earth, being surrounded by countries using it as a dump for oil, mercury, chemical waste, raw sewage and plain household refuse. Beaches are sometimes temporarily closed for health reasons and a UN study suggested that if the pollution continues unchecked, the sea could be technically dead by 2025.

Before leaving for Spain, I'd read an article highlighting the pollution black spots and recommending which types of fish to avoid, mainly shellfish as they tend to exist among the debris on the sea floor. Despite a certain amount of ribbing from everyone else, I stuck to the guidelines during my four trips to the area, and rather smugly was the only member of the crew to avoid any kind of stomach upset.

To view the fight against pollution, we spent a day on board one of the monitoring vessels that trawl the waters with a large pipe collecting samples from various depths. The technicalities were largely lost on me, but the sight of dolphins swimming alongside the ship and leaping the bow wave seemed as good a symbol of hope as any.

Once a week we had a day off, when we relaxed or visited places as ordinary tourists rather than in the frenzied style of our working trips. On our first day off I hired a car and drove to Granada with George to see the Alhambra palace, built in the fourteenth century and one of the finest examples of Moorish architecture. To quote an old Spanish saying, 'There is no greater misfortune in this world than to be blind in Granada.'

The day went well up to the point when George told me to ignore the directions of a traffic cop and we came uncomfortably close to sampling some Spanish porridge. (George's version of events is slightly different - apparently we would have been fine if I'd just slammed the accelerator to the floor while he ducked below the seat.)

Our next free day was spent in Tangier, having crossed over from Gibralter, and although interesting to visit, we were hustled from the moment we left the ferry to the moment we returned. It was clear that if ever we were to film there we would need a constant police escort for both the gear and ourselves. Give me Belfast or Glasgow any day.

One of the major events we covered was an Easter festival at a small fishing village. The day was to begin with a traditional church service, followed by a procession through the streets and ending in the middle of the village with a blessing in a specially constructed garden scene, complete with statue of Mary. As festivals can be pretty chaotic we hired a couple of locals, Pedro and Danielle, supposedly *au fait* with the festivities, to advise us how to organise the filming so that we wouldn't miss any of the highlights. Their 'expertise' turned out to be as extensive as my knowledge of open-heart surgery.

Pedro was a large bear of a man who just seemed to be along for the ride and the chance to devour as much food and drink as was humanly possible. His ambition in life seemed to be to explore the outer limits of human appetite. He was the only person I've met who could eat, drink, smoke, belch and break wind all at the same time, and we soon nicknamed him the Beast. The sight of him smoking while sucking out prawn heads and farting was enough to quell one's appetite for even the most sumptuous of paellas.

We recced the festival site the day before Easter Sunday and in a short space of time had learned as much ourselves as Pedro and Danielle had been able to proffer, at which point we dispensed with their services. I could see Chris, our production manager, breathe a sigh of relief at this major saving to our catering budget.

With just one camera we couldn't hope to cover the whole procession and so we chose some key sites that would allow us to film the beginning, middle and end of the proceedings. By the afternoon the recce was complete and we were looking forward to what was obviously going to be a colourful and dramatic day. The best laid plans of mice and men....

We arrived on Sunday morning to a brilliant sky, a large crowd - and a force eight gale. Remaining upright involved leaning over at forty degrees, while the adjacent beach had been whipped up into a violent sandstorm. Julia took a photograph of George, Mike and myself around the tripod, protected against the wind and sand with anoraks, scarves and goggles, looking like a party of Antarctic explorers who had taken a seriously wrong turn.

It all added a touch of drama to the day's proceedings. Women swathed in black robes struggled valiantly against the howling winds, while cloaks and costumes billowed like sails in the powerful gusts.

The march began with the priest greeting John the Baptist, although his 'peace brother' V-sign was more Spanish Harlem than Spanish Ancient. The procession then got underway and we battled against wind and crowds to grab shots from our chosen vantage points.

The climax of the procession was two groups of young men (representing the Jews and the Sailors) racing each other down the main street, each carrying a large statue of the Virgin Mary on a litter. The resulting spectacle, with the two stampeding teams and their precariously wobbling statues needed only Stuart Hall's frenzied commentary to become a religious *It's A Knockout*.

'And the Sailors are playing their Joker on this game.... oh, and there goes the Virgin Mary!'

The longest and hardest day of our trip also turned out to be the most enjoyable.

We were to spend the day on a fishing trawler, starting at dawn filming the nets being prepared and then following the day's fishing through to selling the catch at the evening markets. The day began on the quayside at four thirty, in darkness and in the middle of a torrential downpour. It didn't bode well for a day at sea.

The fishing started in an unusual way. At six o'clock all the trawlers would meet outside the harbour and line up Le Mans style. At a blast from the hooter of the presiding trawler, they would race off at full speed to claim the best fishing ground for the day; this would vary, depending on the weather and what type of fish was most in demand. As our trawler was by no means the fastest, the captain had reckoned the best bet was to go for gambas, the large prawns of the region. We headed out to sea and in twenty minutes had lost sight of the other vessels.

The trip to the fishing ground took a couple of hours, which we spent relaxing and sharing breakfast with the crew. There are few physically tougher jobs than deep-sea fishing and the crew all looked as hard as teak. What they thought of us with our 'easy-life' hands I have no idea, but we all got on well, particularly when the carafe of rough red wine was handed round as a morning aperitif.

We arrived at about eight o'clock and the crew began their work. Any romantic notions of fishing being largely muscle, sinew and intuition were soon dispelled by the vast array of high-tech equipment and powerful lifting gear that swung into action.

The gambas we were after were half a mile down, just above the sea bed, so the net had to be trawled a mere two or three feet above the sea floor. Any higher and the gambas would be missed, any lower and the net would drag in the sand and rocks and possibly become entangled. But given the size of the net, the area covered and the depths involved, success depended as much on instinct as technology.

By mid-afternoon the nets were ready to be hauled in and the winches began their slow winding, the captain constantly adjusting the boat's speed and position to maintain equal tension on the straining cables. When the net finally surfaced it was swung onto the deck and the day's catch slithered out in all directions. As intended, the catch was mainly gambas, but supplemented by a variety of sea life, most notably large spider crabs measuring up to a foot across - the stuff of nightmares.

We arrived back at port at about seven o'clock and filmed the fish being taken off to market. When the catch was sold, the day was over and the fishermen's work complete. I appreciated the satisfaction they must have got from a job that goes from start to finish in a single day. In stumbling Spanish we thanked the crew and went our separate ways. For us it had been another filming day, typical in its offering of a new experience. For the trawler crew we may have been a slight diversion, but their day had followed a routine that would have been familiar to fishermen a thousand years ago.

To paraphrase Dickens, we arrived in Gibralter at the best of times and the worst of times.

The previous week had seen the shooting of three IRA members by the SAS. The Rock was still buzzing with controversy. Security was high to guard against possible retaliation by the IRA, so our arrival at the border with a van full of equipment caused much consternation.

The Gibraltese police are Spanish in nature, but because the Rock is British they wear British police uniforms. It was a little disconcerting to be approached by what appeared to be your average English bobby, if somewhat suntanned, only to be addressed in a thick Spanish accent. The PC suspiciously viewed the cases in the back of the van.

'Whaas all thees then?' He didn't actually add 'chummy' but I did detect a hint of sarcasm indicative of Hendon Police Training Centre. Maybe they had started correspondence courses in patronising police patter.

'We're from England, here to do some filming with the Army.'

'Ah, the BBC?'

Here we go.

'No - we're a British freelance crew working for an independent production company commissioned by Channel 4 Television with joint funding from several other European television stations.'

It was no good. We'd lost him after the first 'no' denying BBC status. Perhaps if we'd said 'Yes' we would have sailed straight through, but as it was, cases were opened, details noted and our names run through the security computer. After half an hour we were allowed to continue, but I resolved next time to claim Auntie's patronage and use it for all it was worth.

We stayed at the Rock Hotel, the largest and most sumptuous in the colony and a throwback to the days of the Empire. Enjoying an evening drink on the leafy veranda, with the strains of a military band floating up from the barracks below and the sun setting slowly over the horizon, was probably as close as one could get to the days when a globe was largely pink.

Also staying at the hotel was a crew from Thames Television. They were making the documentary *Death On The Rock* that was later to cause so much controversy. Their filming had been going well, in fact a little too well because their supply of film was getting dangerously low.

On our first evening Geoff was approached in the bar by the director of the Thames crew. After the usual 'hail-fellow-well-met-we're-all-pros-together' pleasantries, the director mentioned his shortage of film. Having seen our stock of carefully chilled cans, the director asked if they could borrow some, to be replaced later by supplies currently in transit from England. Geoff was sympathetic, but explained that because the replacement batch of film would not have been tested by us before leaving England, using it would nullify our insurance cover. (All major films have negative insurance i.e. should there turn out to be a problem with the film stock, then the insurance company will pay the cost of a reshoot, but only if a sample of the stock has been tested beforehand.) The hail-fellow manner cooled somewhat, but no more was said and we assumed that was the end of the matter.

The following morning, however, the request was made again, but this time by the Thames presenter, all smiles and charm. By now it was clear that they were fairly desperate and as our stock of film was kept in a hotel storeroom, we became aware how vulnerable it was to being 'borrowed'. Current affairs crews on a 'hot' story tend to shoot first and ask questions later (a bit like the SAS), so as a precaution Chris quietly moved our supply of tins to his room. All's fair in love, war and film-making. It may have seemed churlish not to help fellow professionals, but we couldn't jeopardise our own project. In the end the Thames programme was completed using their own film, so perhaps they'd been worrying unduly.

Our own filming concentrated on the colony's military significance for the episode on warfare in the series. This required the co-operation of the resident forces. The army has always tended to regard film crews with initial mistrust, probably viewing them as dangerous long-haired pinko lefties. However, once you have convinced them that you are not about to threaten 'national security' or portray them as merciless killers, they are only too keen to help. Overly keen, in fact, as there is nothing the military enjoys more than showing off its toys.

And what toys.

On the first morning we were given our very own Nimrod aircraft and crew to play with, complete with all working parts. This was a considerable step-up from flying kites on Parliament Hill.

'OK, that was fine but could you give us another overhead pass, this time much lower and with full engine power?'

It was like asking Benny Hill if he would mind doing a sketch with half-a-dozen Page Three models.

One of the other toys was a Lynx helicopter. I knew how manoeuvrable a small commercial helicopter could be, and assumed that these larger craft would be rather cumbersome. I stood corrected and open-mouthed in awe as the pilot performed stunts that made our crop-spraying Alfonso seem like the apocryphal old lady on her Sunday drive.

OK, if you play with toys long enough, eventually you are going to break them. This applies as much to the army as to any destructive three-year old, except on this occasion the toy was a ceremonial gun with a range of six miles. The sergeant showing us the army's pride and joy was obviously having as much fun as our other demonstrators. So much so that at one point he lost concentration and a hydraulic steel arm swept down, neatly slicing off the foot-long, two-inch brass handle protruding from the back of the gun. He didn't seem that bothered, probably happened all the time. Bit of superglue and she'd be right as rain.

After a few programmes with the military I realised that the services can be a sanctuary for someone who is not really cut out for civilian life. But sometimes you come across someone who doesn't fit into the military either.

Such a character was Joe.

I guess he would normally be described as short and powerfully built. In actual fact he was square. Five foot two in any direction. And all of it muscle.

Joe had had a somewhat chequered career with the army. Sometimes he was on a charge for assault, sometimes he wasn't. His history seemed to be one of longish periods of steady but unspectacular progress, interspersed with short and spectacular periods of violence, usually against a senior NCO. He would then be busted back to private to start the long haul back to conformity and promotion to lance-corporal. This yo-yo existence didn't please him, but he seemed resigned to his military lot, even though there appeared to be no particular niche into which he could fit. Until he discovered caving.

Being a caving aficionado in Gibralter is like being a chocoholic in Cadbury's. The Rock is riddled with tunnels and caves, both man-made and natural, and with the army's blessing Joe took it upon himself to explore each and every one. This compromise not only kept Joe in the army and gainfully employed, but also out of sight and harm's way. I half suspected however that his superiors were secretly hoping that one day Joe would simply head off underground and never reappear.

Joe's new vocation suited him down to the ground (sorry, I couldn't resist that) and he was appointed our official guide to the subterranean world of Gibralter. We scrambled after him down steep gullies and through tiny openings, and I marvelled how someone so squat could slip so effortlessly through the narrowest of gaps.

Having completed our filming, we made our way back to the surface, blinking like moles in the glare of the sunlight. We had lunch with Joe and heard Barrack Room Theory No. 19 about the SAS incident before packing up our gear to head back across the border into Spain.

As we approached the border guards I prepared myself for the inevitable.

'Are you the BBC?'

'Er, well, yes, sort of. Yes, we are the BBC - BBC Channel 4.'

What's a Greek urn (and other tragedies)

The Spanish trip had been a success: we'd completed the shooting schedule, ended up with a good local crew and been well looked after by Federico, who had coped with the logistics of transport, accommodation, locations and filming permits. Now well blooded as a team, we felt confident that we could cope with any problems Greece was likely to throw our way.

Wrong.

Everything that had gone well in Spain went badly in Greece, partly due to our Greek contacts but mainly because sometimes things just go awry (I think it's called 'life'). Then, almost as a final gesture, fate threw in a personal tragedy. As an example of how filming abroad is not all wine and roses Greece was a textbook case.

We descended through the smog into Athens Airport. For all its claim to being the birthplace of Western culture and its blue sky/white marble postcard image, Athens, to be blunt, stinks. It has a pollution problem that makes Los Angeles look like GHQ Greenpeace. A perpetual yellow haze hangs over the city; combined with the heat of the Greek summer it creates a cocktail that annually kills many of the city's frail and elderly. The Japanese trend for bottled oxygen would do a roaring trade.

The pollution is so bad that it has begun to corrode Athens' greatest treasure and main tourist attraction, the Acropolis. What it did to our lungs I shudder to think. The main culprit is the choking extra-high-lead-content fumes that pour out of the million or so cars, buses and trucks that daily clog the streets of the capital. If you want to appreciate just how wonderfully calm, free-flowing and easy-going London traffic is, try driving through Athens at 3 a.m. on a Sunday morning. Within twenty minutes you'll be pining for Hyde Park Corner on a rainy Monday morning with road works in Piccadilly.

After landing and clearing customs we met the Greek contingent who were to be our guides, drivers and general fixers for the next five weeks. In charge was George, late twenties, tall, thin, bearded and somewhat intense, who spoke flawless English (his mother was English). His assistant was Nicos, a quiet unassuming local who apparently spoke no English, but nevertheless gave the impression of understanding all that was going on around him.

We gathered all the equipment and trooped out to the car park, where we met our first disappointment. For a vehicle that was to be transporting us and the gear for hundreds of hot and dusty miles over the next five weeks it left a lot to be desired. Basically a small and rather battered camper van, it looked as if it had done one too many runs across Europe for Club 18-30. George seemed quite proud of his offering.

'I put a fridge in the back for your film stock.'

Indeed he had, but as it took up all the available space we had to pull it out before filling the van to the last available inch with our gear. Result: one miffed George, one miffed crew, one bad start.

We crawled our way through Athens' perpetual rush hour. Ancient buildings were crumbling for the sake of modern transport, yet we were barely moving. Not much to show for 2,000 years of progress.

The next morning I was relieved to discover that we would be leaving Athens and heading for Hydra, one of the many islands that dot the waters of the Aegean. Even better, we were going by hydrofoil, Russian-built and still one of the fastest seagoing passenger transports in the world.

We arrived at the quayside with our silver gear boxes. Normally when travelling with equipment, arrangements are made beforehand to accommodate the cases but today that seemed to have been overlooked. Chris blamed George, George denied ever being asked, so we ended up battling with the locals and tourists over the limited seats and baggage space. Boarding became a farce as we tried to load twenty pieces of luggage along the narrow gangplank, hassled by both the ticket collector and the other passengers. Hail fellow, well met, get that case outa my face. I've had easier times in a rush hour tube.

Despite several threats from the ticket collector that we would be thrown off, we managed to load all the gear and find somewhere to sit. Travelling across the sparkling waters at high speed was exhilarating. In the weeks to come we were to make several sea journeys on a variety of craft, and all but one were highlights of the trip.

On arriving at Hydra we went through the same experience unloading, though this time to the delight of all and sundry - they were getting rid of us. Yea, you *and* your mother!

Having piled all the cases on the quayside, we looked around for our vehicle.

'Er, George, isn't there a van for the gear?'

'Vehicles aren't allowed.'

Stupid of me to ask.

'So how do we get all this lot to the hotel?'

'Local transport.'

'But you just said....'

George nodded to a man approaching some twenty yards away - with a couple of donkeys.

I stood back as the local transport executive loaded his two trusty steeds with an alarming array of cases, but the animals seemed not to notice the weight and just continued chewing in their nosebags. With us carrying the few remaining pieces of luggage, we set off along the cobbled streets up the hill to our small hotel. My knowledge of working with donkeys was a little limited and I wondered how we were going to get along. I had vague childhood memories of riding them along the beach at Whitley Bay but this was my first experience of professional collaboration.

The cool interior of the hotel was a relief from the heat of the day and I began reducing the camera equipment to essentials. Using the animals for a leisurely walk up from the quayside was one thing, but relying on them as a filming vehicle was another. I decided that we would be best served by a close relation of theirs, shanks's pony (i.e. our own two feet, for those of you born outside the North-East).

By the time I'd finished I had the kit down to the camera and tripod, a lens case and my accessories bag, more than enough to lug around but the least we could get away with.

That afternoon we did some general shots of the harbour, but our main aim was to film the local yacht race from the island back to Athens the next morning.

Staying on an island with no motor traffic I'd expected the day to begin with the gentle sound of sea lapping against the shoreline. Well, yes, the sea did lap - accompanied by every waking cat, dog, cockerel and donkey in the district, plus the church bells and, as the aural *pièce de résistance*, the call to prayer blasting out over the town's public address system. I'd had quieter mornings back in London waking up to my neighbours playing Bob Marley at a million zigawatts. After the all-night drone from the hotel generator, the dawn chorus was the fitting climax to a lousy night. We got up, ready to face the day, totally wrecked.

After breakfast at one of the terrace cafes overlooking the bay we climbed above the harbour to film the start of the race, a classic travel-brochure shot of bobbing white sails on a sparkling sea. Then a dash back to the hotel to collect our belongings for the journey back to Athens. We grabbed a couple of passing donkeys outside the hotel and returned to the quayside to hail a cab - no, you didn't misread that. The water taxis operate just like their landlubber cousins, providing a quick alternative to the scheduled sailings between the islands. And you are spared a marine version of the cabbie's patter.

''Ere, you'll never guess who I 'ad in my boat last week.... nah, sorry, I can't help you wiv them cases 'cos I did me back in hauling up the anchor.'

As we sped back towards Athens all the hassles of the outward journey, the local transport and the sleepless night dissolved in the refreshing spray - if you are island hopping taxis are definitely the only way to travel. Consequently we arrived back revived and in good time to cover the end of the race. After a shaky start we felt we were back on track.

The following day was spent around Athens, logging the obligatory shots of the Parthenon before heading off to Corinth to sail down the ship canal. Built in 1893 across the isthmus joining the Peloponnese and mainland Greece, the canal is notable for the dizzying height of its walls, accentuated by its narrowness and arrow-straight four miles of waterway. We had planned to film one of the larger ships that scrape through with merely inches to spare and arrived just in time - to see it disappear out of the far end. Having driven two hours to catch the only big vessel that afternoon it was a perfect example of bad timing.

We sailed through the canal ourselves but in a much smaller vessel. Being dwarfed by the sheer walls rising a hundred or so feet above us on either side was an eerie feeling - we were completely out of touch with the land above. The canal was one enormous stone bath and we were the plastic duck.

The next day it was back to Hydra to cover another event, this time the island's summer festival. Covering any festivity in the midst of hundreds of revellers presents endless unforeseen difficulties and the filming process is inevitably chaotic. Keeping track of performers and events in an ever-changing programme is challenging enough. Then there are the physical problems of lugging the equipment around in a large crowd and trying to get a clapperboard on each shot. And when you add stroppy security guards and people blocking the camera, you end up with a form of filming known as KBS - Kick, Bollock and Scramble.

From my perspective it is probably the most difficult type of filming. One has to be totally mobile yet totally self-sufficient, carrying all the accessories needed to cope with any eventuality. Lenses, filters, batteries, magazines, camera covers, tins of stock and black changing bag for loading film - all have to be to hand. You have to grab any chance to reload a magazine, even on the ground with hundreds of people milling past - and you just pray that the cameraman doesn't suddenly move off while you're in mid-load. All very manic and a bit tense at times, but afterwards very satisfying to sit down and know that you've coped with a difficult situation.

On this occasion we were provided with some local help to assist in ferrying and guarding the equipment during the festival. Pan was a five-foot Vietnam veteran with a huge bushy beard and of similar stature to our Gibraltar caving corporal, Joe. I began to wonder whether spending long periods in the army was responsible for stunting, or even rearranging one's growth.

Pan had obviously decided that he'd had enough of the Marines/Special Services/Catering Corps or whatever, and had opted to kick back and spend the rest of his life in the Greek isles. We gave him the task of carrying the tripod wherever we went, a cinch, I figured, after tackling Charlie in the Vietnamese jungle. However I hadn't reckoned on his local celebrity status.

As we moved through the crowds I would look around for him and he'd be greeting yet another table of drinking mates, while up ahead Mike and the camera were vanishing among the crowds. I had to keep dropping back and hauling Pan away from his revelry, torn between losing Mike or Pan - or both. At the end of an exhausting day I was thankful that I hadn't had to keep track of him in the jungle.

By the second week of filming, the logistics of the trip were beginning to strain relationships between the Greeks and British. We would often visit two or three locations in a day and it was simply not feasible to take all the vehicles and every piece of luggage and equipment to every location.

So some days there were three groups setting off at different times. First off was the van, leaving at five or earlier with the equipment needed for the morning location. At a more civilised hour the filming crew would then fly or go by water taxi to rendezvous with the van. Meanwhile the production team would leave with the rest of the equipment and our personal luggage to meet us at the afternoon location. Inevitably a piece of equipment or luggage would sometimes be sent with the wrong crew, requiring Nicos on one occasion to drive through the night to retrieve a case for the morning's filming.

To make matters worse, George and Nicos seemed unaware of what we required as a documentary crew needing to shoot in specific and often exclusive locations. They seemed to regard us more like a group of tourists. The camper van was too small for all the kit and unsuitable for the country roads, yet the only alternative George had offered was a clapped-out old bus. Whenever we travelled by boat or plane no arrangements were made for the equipment, so our arrival at check-in always created havoc. Then we would turn up at locations that were either unsuitable, or for which filming permits had not been arranged, or to which we'd been given no more access than the general public, and so would end up behind barriers fighting for space among busloads of sightseers.

On one occasion we'd just lined up a shot of an ancient temple when an English tourist with his handicam video planted himself directly in front of our camera. He then announced in broad Yorkshire 'Right, Ah'm goin' to get a shot o' this', the sub-text of which was clearly 'Tha' bloody professional buggers thinks tha' can come dahn here and shove us arahnd - well Ah's paid me money and Ah'll stands where Ah bloody well likes'.

The English abroad, you gotta luv 'em.

As the second week progressed the catalogue of chaos seemed to grow daily: interviewees would not turn up as arranged, we would arrive too late to catch an important one-off event, a supposedly prebooked flight would turn out not to have been booked.

During the post-mortems, Geoff (director) and Chris (production manager) would accuse George of not having made the arrangements as planned, while George would retort that he was suddenly being asked for flights, locations and filming permits that had not been previously mentioned. While there may indeed have been a certain amount of misunderstanding, it seemed that George and Nicos had neither the experience to cope with the schedule nor the political clout needed to obtain the permits we required.

Consequently the trip descended into a saga of increasing tension between the two teams, with flare-ups and losses of temper, usually followed by partial reconciliations because each side needed the other to get the job done. Behind the scenes Geoff became increasingly distrustful of George and tried to organise another fixer to replace him, but in the end was unable to find anyone with George's local knowledge and bilingual abilities.

Mike, George (our sound recordist) and myself remained apart from the disputes as we had no involvement with the logistics of the trip, and were left merely to spectate on the developing conflict. Every day began with us wondering whether George had walked off the job because of yet another argument with Geoff, or Chris, or both. On one memorable morning we left the hotel to drive to a shipyard to film an important launching, unaware that our fixer had been left behind. He arrived in a taxi fifteen minutes later and immediately proceeded to have a blazing full-volume row with Chris in the middle of the yard. The trip was becoming a real-life soap.

As if this was not enough, one of our drivers, Costas, had been displaying a typically laid-back Greek-island approach to the job, which was OK for driving around holiday-makers but not for our schedule. His continual unpunctuality in the mornings was creating problems and after several warnings he eventually went the way of Victor, our Spanish driver, and was similarly replaced by an older man who got on with the job with the minimum of fuss.

The international friction finally came to a head during a long journey that we made to Naxos, one of the more distant islands. The trip was to take about four hours and the plan was for the film crew to leave early evening, arrive about ten o'clock and check into a local hotel. George and Nicos were to arrive the next afternoon.

The skipper of our small craft had obviously been to the Captain Bligh Finishing School for Seafarers (which is probably why he didn't have any crew). Despite the exorbitant fee he was being paid, he made his dislike of us abundantly clear, even refusing us a cup of coffee from the cabin stores. Nevertheless the journey was enjoyable and sitting on deck watching a spectacular sunset made me yearn for my days as a budding accountant.

True to schedule, at about ten o'clock we pulled into a small bay and I started to get the gear ready to go ashore. Then the captain went to bed. We were still about a hundred yards from shore and were obviously going no further. We didn't know where we were. It certainly wasn't Naxos. We settled down as best we could in the cramped quarters of the wheelhouse (no captain's cabin for us).

At six in the morning we were woken by the sound of the anchor being lifted and the engines being gunned. We then spent a further four hours travelling before arriving at our destination, now some twelve hours late. Another nail in the schedule's coffin. Having paid George to arrange the trip, our production team felt that he'd simply got the cheapest boat available, irrespective of how long it would take to make the journey.

When George and Nicos arrived later in the day they denied knowing how long the trip would be, but the feeling that we had literally been taken for a ride by a couple of hustlers boiled over. Nicos walked out and headed back to Athens. This came as something of a shock - he had always been the quiet one of the partnership. Obviously matters had been brewing behind the scenes and this was the final straw for him.

With Nicos gone there was some doubt whether George would remain, but presumably the settlement fee at the end of the job was too tempting to dismiss and he elected to stay.

The fiasco of the overnight trip also produced an encounter between the two Georges. George the Sound had long had his suspicions that George the Greek had been pulling a few fast ones and decided to vent his feelings.

Showtime.

'Quite a journey we had last night, George.'

'Oh really?'

'Supposed to get in about ten but didn't arrive until this morning.'

'So I heard.'

'Amazing no one knew how long it would take.'

'Is that so?'

''Course, a real local guide would have known.'

'Meaning what, exactly?'

(Gloves off)

'Meaning if you weren't such a useless pillock we'd have got here on time!'

At this point I intervened before blows were struck. Although entertaining, it was the watershed for Anglo-Greek relations.

The remaining days ground on but despite the problems, the tins of exposed stock kept piling up. We were making progress but at times it felt like swimming through treacle.

The sea trips were always a welcome break from the long journeys in the camper van. One highlight was filming a modern replica of a trireme, an ancient Greek warship with three ranks of oarsmen on each side. I doubt whether the authenticity went as far as lashing the crew, but at full speed with all oars in unison it was magnificent testimony to the glory of the ancient Greek navy.

We returned to port and started unloading our equipment on to the quayside. A passing yacht hailed us.

'Hallo please BBC?'

By now I was used to this. I merely tipped my cap for the inquirer to read his own answer.

With only a few days left we felt that we had broken the back of the trip and the worst was over. Not so. While filming one morning at one of the temples around Athens, Chris appeared looking pale and shaken. He'd just taken a phone message that Geoff's son in England had suddenly died. Geoff left immediately and we completed the remaining schedule without him. It was a cruel end to what had been a generally unhappy trip.

A few days later we said goodbye to George at Athens Airport, both sides trying to be pleasant to each other but relieved that it was all over.

In retrospect, it would have been easy to dismiss George and Nicos as a couple of locals on the make with a foreign crew on a large budget. However I felt that they weren't so much hustlers as simply lacking the experience and influence necessary for such a job. Hence ultimately I was prepared to give them the benefit of the doubt.

Several days after returning home we discovered that among their expense claims was one for petrol - on Hydra.

Turkish delights

Before I arrived in Istanbul, the sum total of my knowledge of Turkey and its culture had been gleaned from watching *Midnight Express* and those klutzy old ads for Fry's Turkish Delight. Consequently I assumed Istanbul would be peopled by sadistic overweight bisexual male chocaholics and scantily clad belly dancers who never quite make it to the seventh veil. What I discovered was, as they say in the best travelogues, 'a city of contrast, changeless yet ever changing'.

The only city in the world to straddle two continents, Istanbul also straddles two eras of civilisation. The old traditions of the bazaar, the mosques and the near-deification of past leaders clash garishly with the face of modern Istanbul: chic fashion, office blocks and a nine-lane highway, signs of a country desperately trying to break into the economic goldmine of the EU.

As we arrived at the airport and approached the inevitable hassle with customs, I suddenly remembered the small sachets of silica gel crystals in each equipment case, designed to absorb the condensation that occurs in warm climates. My Turkish guide book was brimming with useful phrases for when one should find oneself 'At The Hotel', 'At The Beach' or 'At The Nightclub' ('Would you like to dance or would your three brothers like to turn me into a shish kebab?'), but somewhat lacking when it came to being 'At The Airport Customs Desk With Small Sachets Of Unidentified Crystals Lurking In The Bottom Of One's Luggage'.

The Giorgio Moroder theme in *Midnight Express* that had accompanied Billy Hayes' chase through the back streets of Istanbul drummed in my brain as we approached the moustached sentinels of the customs department (*every* man at the airport seemed to be sporting a moustache - I expected to see a banner proclaiming 'Istanbul Welcomes Fans of the Village People'). In fact the examination was perfunctory;

perhaps they were more concerned with drugs going out of the country than stuff coming in. I made a mental note to ditch the sachets discreetly before we left: 'Psst, you wanna buy any silica, man?'

After clearing customs we met our local guide, Esme, a pleasant-faced girl in her early twenties. By western standards she would have been deemed overweight, but judging by the admiring looks she drew from every male we passed, she was obviously the Claudia Schiffer of Turkish womanhood. (Although with bisexuality fairly common among the city's premarital men, I'm not sure if it was just Esme they were admiring. Perhaps I was the Turkish delight.)

Our two drivers were a couple of male students, the real McCoy of Young Turks. Given the track record of our previous younger drivers I wondered how long these two would last. Perhaps it would have been kinder to fire them at once: 'Look guys, nothing personal but to save you a load of hassle in the next couple of weeks maybe you should quit while you're ahead.'

My instincts about their future employment prospects seemed well founded, as our drive from the airport was straight out of *Days Of Thunder*. A nine-lane highway runs through the middle of Istanbul and although I didn't actually see anyone on the sidelines with a stopwatch and pit crew, the motorway was obviously Turkey's answer to the Indy 500. It's always easy to make cracks about foreign drivers, but the sheer speed and lane-changing bravado of our own Tom Cruise made my past encounters with Hyde Park Corner seem like a Sunday drive through Little Piddling on the Mire. I figured that the Turkish Highway Code had to be the World's Shortest Book. I didn't see any pedestrians, probably for the simple reason that there were none left.

By the time we arrived at the hotel my knuckles had welded themselves into the upholstery and the porter who opened my door was met with a grin of manic terror. Prising myself out of the seat and giving silent thanks in the vague direction of Mecca, I began to help the others unload when we fell foul of the local constabulary. A police officer turned up and in no uncertain terms indicated that we should move our vehicles - clearly impractical, given the lack of alternative parking and the spread of cases on the pavement. Such situations can often be defused by a little tact, patience and diplomacy but George decided not to bother: 'Yea, yea, sure, look, we'll move the cars as soon as we've shifted this lot but in the meantime just get lost and leave us alone.'

I'm not sure how much of this the officer understood, but he retaliated with a flurry of Turkish that in Thames Valley Police parlance probably came out as 'Listen sunshine, if you don't move this bleedin' jam jar pronto you'll be down the nick before you can say "perverted prison practices"'.

The argument was becoming heated and too good an opportunity to miss for one of those never-to-be-forgotten-holiday-snaps-you'll-love-to-pore-over, so I whipped out my camera and caught the two in full flow. Immediately the officer turned his wrath on me. Somewhere in the distance I could hear the faint strains of a public address system: 'The Midnight Express now standing at Platform Five is about to depart....'

The scene was beginning to develop into an embarrassing international incident. I envisaged Our Man in Istanbul being summoned by the Turkish authorities:

'Why do we have your English hooligans? There is no football?'

Fortunately the hotel manager appeared and was able to dissuade the officer from carting us off downtown for a session of Turkish reflexology.

We obviously had some way to go to understand the mysteries of the East.

We began filming in the bazaar that dominates downtown old Istanbul. Basically an enclosed street market, the bazaar was a labyrinth of walkways and side streets, with everyone jostling for space while dodging laden handcarts. It was obviously the inspiration behind the Milton Keynes shopping centre. As we followed our guide through the maze

of alleyways we soon became disorientated, again like
Milton Keynes shopping centre.

We spent the afternoon capturing the sounds and colours
of a market that had probably changed little in several
centuries. We were deep into the bazaar when we met
Princess Michael of Kent - as you do. I knew it was her 'cos
I recognised her from the Cup Final, she being the only royal
who seems vaguely interested in football (you see the Queen
at Wembley from time to time, but you can tell her heart's
not really in it). Or maybe the Rest just keep pulling rank:
'Anyone for the Cup Final? No? Well, we know who'll be
attending that....' So the Princess approaches each May with
a sense of foreboding, knowing that she's going to spend a
whole afternoon stuck next to an ancient FA official, who
always looks like one of those head-of-state interpreters as
they translate the action on the pitch into royalspeak.

A look of alarm passed across her face when she saw us.
Maybe she wasn't supposed to be there at all, having slipped
away from some official function to do a spot of shopping,
but she did a quick about-turn and disappeared down one of
the many side streets.

Next on the filming schedule was a naval parade at a
monument dedicated to a Turkish military leader. Istanbul
seems to have an obsession with the wartime glories of its
past, and statues to leaders of successful campaigns are
dotted all over town like signposts. If you're not sure whom
you're looking at, it's a safe bet that it's either a butch and
barechested bloke called Barbarossa (or Khair-ed-Din to be
precise), or Kemal Atatürk, who led the Turkish forces at
Gallipoli in World War One and went on to become the
country's first president in 1923.

Also known as 'Redbeard' (can't imagine why),
Barbarossa was a sixteenth-century Barbary pirate of no
mean success when it came to whipping foreign fleets. On
the strength of such victories he became admiral of the
Ottoman fleet and enjoyed a celebrated position at court as
general scourge of the infidel.

Four hundred years on and of a similarly sensitive disposition, Atatürk was obviously not one for sympathetic listening, taking things on board or appreciating where people were coming from. His command to his front line troops during World War One was stark and simple.

'I am not ordering you to attack, I am ordering you to die, and when you fall others will come forward to take your place.'

Phew. Obviously one of life's born motivators. I'd hate to play in any football team he was managing.

Atatürk's exploits provided the setting for our programme about Mediterranean warfare. Gallipoli, the European north-west peninsula that forms the Dardanelles Strait with Asian Turkey, was the site of an eleven-month Allied campaign in WWI that cost 500,000 lives on both sides and has become identified with the Australian and New Zealand troops who bore the brunt of the fighting.

The bay where the forces landed became known as Anzac Cove and there, down on the beach, mere yards from the water, lies the Ari Burnu cemetery, a beautifully tended graveyard for the men and boys who fell there. I say 'boys' because there were several in their teens recorded on the headstones. The youngest I saw was only seventeen. I tried to imagine the tragedy of some young kid who had possibly never known anything but life on a farm, being swept up in a wave of patriotic fervour only to die needlessly on this foreign shore thousands of miles from home.

The struggles of that time have also had a lasting impact on the Turks, and a large area where the fighting occurred has been declared a World Peace Park. There are monuments to the fallen of both sides and the thirty-one Turkish and Allied war cemeteries are kept in pristine condition with not a hint of graffiti. I had expected to find the memorials depressing, and while they certainly brought a lump to the throat, they were also uplifting, a testimony to the courage and dedication of those who died.

Each of the countries involved has its own monument but one of the Turks' own memorials, situated in a clearing on

Chunuk Bair hill, is by far the most spectacular. Arranged in a circle of some sixty yards diameter are six enormous stone plaques, each about twenty feet high by forty feet wide and carved with lengthy descriptions of the Gallipoli battles. As large monuments go, the plaques rank with Stonehenge and Easter Island. If no-one knew their origins, they too would be recognised as an extra-terrestrial airport (Terminal 3).

On the top of Chunuk Bair there lies a more simple memorial to the conflict. An area of the Turkish trench system had been restored and nestles cosily among the trees at the top of the steep slopes. In the warm afternoon sunshine it was difficult to imagine the slaughter that must have occurred there, but innumerable battles, including the Falklands, have confirmed the deadly consequences of charging a hilltop trench system.

From Gallipoli we travelled to the ruins of Ephesus, an ancient city on the Aegean coast. Founded in 600 BC, Ephesus has some of the best preserved buildings from an era when Greek civilisation was the most advanced in the world. Unlike many ancient sites - which are often no more than a few broken walls or an outline in the ground - the remains at Ephesus are substantial enough to make you think you are in a living city.

The magnificent main boulevard and wide streets are still fully paved, and lined with the pillared fronts of former buildings. It was easy to imagine toga-wearing intellectuals promenading along the crowded streets, discussing esoteric topics like the meaning of life, the aspirations of mankind and the day's specials in the market.

Among the highlights were the imposing two-storey Library of Celsus and the Temple of Nike, Goddess of Victory and Airborne Souls - or should that be soles? So much for all that 'advanced technological thinking' that went into your trainers. Just goes to show there's nowt new under t'sun, as my old Dad used to say - or might have said, had he been born in Yorkshire.

While filming the temple, we again got embroiled in an argument with a tourist. On this occasion a middle-aged American lady took great umbrage at being asked to stand clear of the temple for all of thirty seconds so that we could do our shot.

'Why the hell should I stay outa the way, I paid my money and I wanna stand here in front of the temple.'

'Yes, but if you could spare us thirty seconds while we get the shot, we'd be most grateful,' pleaded George.

'No way, I wanna get a shot so you guys will have to wait.'

So we waited several minutes while she sorted out her camera, viewed the shot from a variety of different positions, directed her companion through a selection of casual poses before finally taking her snapshot. While aware that we often ask favours of the public when filming on location, people rarely seem to appreciate that we are working, as opposed to just taking a few holiday snaps. The more antagonistic individuals might stop to consider how they would react if someone was similarly obstructive while they were trying to work.

For all its magnificent buildings, the crowning glory of Ephesus is its amphitheatre with seating for an incredible twenty-five thousand. Still perfectly preserved, the back stage is virtually intact, including the original vomitories for entering and exiting the stage. We had special permission to film in the amphitheatre at dawn before the public arrived, and as I walked out of one of the vomitories, the grand sweep of the terraced seating took my breath away. The stage beckoned. This was too good an opportunity to miss:

> *Now is the winter of our discontent*
> *Made glorious summer by this sun of York,*
> *And all the clouds that lower'd upon our house....*

Even my hackneyed delivery of Shakespeare's lines seemed to be lent dramatic power by the majesty of the arena. I don't know if I got the part but they said they'd let me know.

We assembled the camera gear and started to climb the terraces for the grand vista shot of the sun coming up over the city. Halfway up a quick flash of movement on the step above me revealed a coiled snake, little pleased at being woken from its slumbers. (I know, it does seem incredible that it chose to sleep through my Richard III.)

Whenever this happens in the movies, someone always says, 'Don't move!' - so I didn't. Then some flash character usually produces a Colt 45 and blasts the creature into small pieces. What you are supposed to do when armed solely with a lens case, I'm not sure; so I tried to quell my rising panic, stood still and let the snake have the next move. Fortunately it didn't seem to be feeling vindictive and slithered away along the terraces, presumably to wait for the first unsuspecting person off the morning's tourist buses.

The terraces also produced another of nature's less cuddly creatures, a large hornet, although thankfully passed on to the next life, probably to return as a tax inspector. I'd never seen a hornet and so had no appreciation of either their size or potential danger, but if you imagine a wasp about two inches long with a sting like a quarter-inch hypodermic then you know why to avoid stirring up one of their nests.

After two such omens of danger, I was beginning to think that perhaps the Gods were displeased at our presence. The stalls probably weren't too happy about us either. But we managed to set up the camera without further portents and were able to capture the greatest light show on earth - sunrise.

We had a day off in Izmir, about thirty miles north of Ephesus, so George and I wandered around the markets. At one point I lost him, but he reappeared around a corner some twenty minutes later followed by a small grinning boy laden down with two large Turkish carpets.

'What on earth are you going to do with those?' I asked, aware that we still had ten days to go in Turkey followed by two weeks in Egypt, and more than enough luggage to load on and off boats, planes, vans and buses.

'Souvenirs, of course,' replied George triumphantly, obviously pleased at the bargain he'd struck.

'But how are you going to travel with them? We've got enough stuff as it is.'

'Oh, we'll just tie them up and carry them with the gear, not to worry.'

Never can see the wider picture, that's my problem. My attitude towards souvenirs had been fairly practical. Besides the photos I took with my own camera I felt little inclined to burden myself with the usual stuff on offer. George, however, had a more romantic approach.

'Even if it is only tourist stuff, every time you look at it, you remember something about the trip.' In the end I gave in and set about hunting for a carpet to grace my humble flat back in London.

Being a regular patron of Southwark markets, I prided myself on my eye for a bargain. So over the next few hours we became experts on the pros and pitfalls of Turkish-carpet buying, learning to distinguish pure wool from synthetic, shoddy from quality and reasonably-priced from extortionate.

So by the end of the afternoon I was the proud owner of a sumptuous, deep-pile patterned carpet, while George had added yet another to his collection. We returned to the hotel in triumph, where we were greeted by Esme, who viewed our spoils with thinly-disguised amusement.

'Why have you bought these?' she laughed. 'These are just for ripping off tourists.'

'But look at the quality,' we insisted, indignant at this slur on our consumer savvy.

'My uncle makes much better carpets, all hand-made rather than these machine-woven ones and with the discount I can get you, the price will be about the same.'

Our hope that this was some kind of family scam was dashed when Esme took us to her uncle's stall. He showed us a range of exquisite rugs, luxuriously soft and vastly superior to the stiff-backed creations with which we were now lumbered. Having bided his time, Mike purchased a sumptuous kilim which folded easily into his suitcase, while George and I spent the next three weeks looking like a couple of door-to-door carpet salesmen.

You're never far from Islam in Istanbul. The many superb mosques dominate the city's skyline and the calls to prayer boom out from speakers all over the city several times a day. The first call is around dawn and we grew wearily accustomed to being woken each morning by the amplified wailing.

Filming in a mosque presents many difficulties, not least keeping a heavy metal tripod off your shoeless feet. The fairly relaxed attitude that exists among the English public to church services is a world away from the atmosphere inside a large mosque with several hundred worshippers. In most mosques you are made painfully aware that not only are you not welcome, but that your presence will be tolerated only to a minor degree.

The key to capturing prayers on film is to know what is going to happen, as there is little space in a crowded mosque for moving around. At various points during the service, everyone stands up briefly before kneeling down again to prostrate themselves on the intricately designed personal prayer mats. So if you are in one part of the mosque and wish to get somewhere else, you wait for the worshippers to rise for a few seconds and then run between the lines of devotees to your next filming position. Trying to quickly move a camera and tripod between ranks of the faithful with only inches to spare and without treading on their prayer mats proved virtually impossible. As the prayers continued, we drew several fearsome looks and afterwards outside the mosque we were castigated by several of the worshippers for our seeming lack of respect.

'How would you feel if we came in and insulted your religion right in front of you?' demanded one elderly man. There was little we could do but apologise and hope that we hadn't jeopardised the rest of our stay in the city.

After the crowded mosques and tightly-packed streets, it was a relief to board a boat for an afternoon sail down the Bosphorus. We cruised along with Europe on our left and Asia on our right. Having afternoon tea while sailing under the only bridge in the world to span two continents was one in the eye for the Ritz.

On our last afternoon in Istanbul, we headed along the coast to film the harvesting of the live sponges that cling to the rocks just off shore. Arriving at the kind of secluded bay that you see only in travel brochures, our fishing smack anchored in the brilliant turquoise waters. The sponges were at a depth of about ten feet, so the boat's divers just snorkelled down and deposited them in a large net under the boat.

After half an hour the net was hauled aboard and its contents spilled on to the deck. A collection of large, slimy, black objects slithered around revoltingly. They were disgusting. My romantic notion of acquiring a freshly-caught, yellow sponge for my morning ablutions was dashed. I wouldn't have used one of these for cleaning the toilet, let alone my body. Although later assured that after drying and cleaning, the sponges would indeed end up as expected, the moment was gone. So much for the harvest of the seas.

We left Turkey with many impressions of its culture and religion, but as so often happens, it is the small, quirky events that provide the most vivid memories.

The town of Selcuk lies close to the ruins at Ephesus and its museum boasts many treasures from the site. We were setting up some lights for a wide shot of a statue, but one of the lamps needed to be rigged higher than any of our stands would allow. There was a suitable perch for the light in a corner of the ceiling, but we had no means of reaching it without a ladder. I decided to give George a leg-up so that he could stand on my shoulders to rig the light.

With George wobbling precariously overhead we must have resembled a third-rate acrobatic troupe, when from around a corner emerged an elderly man. He watched us for a few seconds before challenging in broad Yorkshire tones (why is it always Yorkshire?)

'Er, excuse me lads, but are you from t'BBC?'

George, can you move those pyramids to the left?

At the time of our trip to Egypt, the most we were likely to suffer was the attentions of an over-zealous souvenir seller or the dramatic effects of the local drinking water. The turmoil of the Middle East seemed to have little relevance to a settled country that had developed a thriving tourist trade and was generally welcoming and friendly. So we had few worries as we flew into Cairo to experience one of the oldest cultures on earth, blissfully unaware of the impact that the shockwaves from the Arab-Israeli conflict were to have on the trip.

As the birthplace of one of the world's first civilisations (dating from at least 4,000 BC), Egypt was to be a key element in the series, having inspired Mediterranean trade, culture and navigation - as well as a rash of Hollywood sand-and-sandal epics.

If you've ever suffered Gatwick airport during a peak-season strike by Air Traffic Control, then you have but sampled the merest sensation of Cairo airport on a lazy Sunday afternoon. Everything takes place in one large hangar; shouting and chaos the norm. After the usual battles with customs we met our local contact, Hasan, who welcomed us with an unusually large production team - there were fifteen of them. Not wishing to appear unfriendly, I went to each one in turn and introduced myself with a smile and a handshake. I later discovered that they were the airport baggage handlers.

Outside the airport we were presented with our transport to the hotel. Although the crew would be travelling in a minibus, the equipment was to go in the back of a decrepit open truck. The camera kit was personally owned by Mike and normally the lovingly maintained camera, lenses and accessories travelled only in his equally immaculate Volvo Estate (I scratched the petrol cap once when filling the tank and I don't think he's ever really forgiven me). So the prospect of the silver cases being bounced around in the back of a dusty old truck was a bit like asking a new Mum if Junior could be strapped to the roof rack.

We padded each case as best we could before tying the whole lot down with an array of ropes that could have doubled as a driftnet. The drive to the hotel was without incident (which in Egyptian traffic terms means that we didn't crash and burst into flames), but as I chatted to Mike during the journey I sensed that spiritually he was in the back of the truck, spread-eagled over his beloved cases.

The Meridien Hotel sits bang in the middle of Cairo, overlooking the Nile. As luxury hotels go it was somewhere in the stratosphere, far better than what we were used to, but the choice was largely determined by the need to keep us well enough to work. The hazards of the local water meant that for visiting Westerners, the Egyptian equivalent of Delhi Belly was just a washed salad or iced drink away. The Meridien, however, was one of only four hotels in Cairo to boast its own water treatment plant, thus hopefully keeping us on the go - or rather not.

Our first day in Egypt was actually a day off and so we grabbed the opportunity to act like tourists and visit the museum and the bazaar. The main attraction of the museum was the Tutankhamen treasures, which had virtually brought London to a standstill on their visit several years earlier. I'd missed out on that occasion and so was looking forward to experiencing them on their home turf.

In a small quiet side room, with apparently no guards or security other than a glass display cabinet, were the 3,000 year-old treasures of the boy king. None of the photographs nor any hype can do them justice, least of all to their crowning glory, the innermost of the three burial caskets, nearly two hundred and fifty pounds of solid gold artwork. Compared to the security for the Mona Lisa in the Louvre, the arrangements for protecting arguably the greatest treasure in the world seemed a joke. Though I suppose if you did steal it, finding a fence might prove a little tricky.

After the museum we headed off to the old bazaar. Like the bazaar in Istanbul, the market in Cairo assails the senses with a barrage of noise, smells and colours. Being on tourist duty I couldn't resist buying a 'fez' or 'tarboosh' and in doing so discovered instant celebrity status, as the tarboosh is an extremely formal piece of headgear. My wearing it in a market was akin to an Egyptian wandering down the Old Kent Road in top hat and tails.

The following day we headed off to our first location, a high-angle view of a church with the harbour in the background, and met the person who was to dominate our two-week stay in Egypt. Ali, a balding civil servant, was the Government minder appointed to ensure that we didn't photograph anything of a sensitive security nature. As we weren't planning to film any military bases we didn't foresee a problem, but it transpired that virtually everything we pointed the camera at seemed to arouse Ali's ire, followed by a blunt refusal to allow filming.

As each shot was lined up, Ali would look down the viewfinder and make some objection, usually because of a ship, bridge or public building in the distant background.

By lunchtime we had barely managed to squeeze off a couple of shots of the church, each with a severely cropped background, and it was clear that the remainder of the trip was in jeopardy if this degree of scrutiny was to continue. We felt there was some other reason to Ali's objections, but when Geoff and Chris asked him what the real problem was, he was vague and evasive. All we could do was carry on and hope that the situation would sort itself out.

The afternoon began with a visit to the local shipyard, but this ended up being a fruitless attempt to record anything other than empty quaysides or close-ups of ropes, chains and anchors. Battles with foreign officialdom were nothing new and on previous trips we had had an occasional run-in, but this was something different.

Worse still, most mornings Ali was accompanied by an ever-changing group of fellow civil servants, and the first two hours would be spent locked in intense negotiations about what exactly we were going to be allowed to film.

At the end of a frustrating first week we had achieved little. Ali, however, was beginning to relax somewhat, and seemed to realise there was nothing sinister in our intentions. Finally, over a conspiratorial coffee, he spilt the beans. Before our arrival, Geoff had hired an Israeli researcher to help prepare material for filming. Despite the official peace between Israel and Egypt, the wounds of previous conflicts had not yet fully healed, so the appearance of an 'enemy' researcher was enough to set Egyptian security alarm bells jangling. Ali was told to be as obstructive as possible, ideally to prevent us shooting anything at all.

With the truth out at last, the situation improved a little. While we still had to be careful when other minders were around, on the days when it was solely Ali we could film virtually whatever we wished. Sometimes he even argued our case against objections from his fellow minders. We realised he trusted us completely when he revealed that he wanted to visit London for a hair transplant.

Clearly here was a man with nothing to hide.

I'd imagined the pyramids to be way out in the desert (which obviously they originally were), but Cairo's urban sprawl is such that they now provide an interesting feature to a few back gardens.

By chance we arrived on one of the country's feast days, when anyone brave (or foolhardy) enough is allowed to climb the pyramids. I was tempted to have a go, but on hearing of the deaths of several past climbers I decided not to tangle with any lingering curses.

For all the pyramids' impressive exteriors, the internal burial chambers were plain and disappointing, long bereft of the treasures they once contained. However, around the three pyramids (Cheops, Chephren and Menkure) there were several tombs for families and close friends of the pharaohs, all offering better displays of paintings and hieroglyphics.

One set of carvings that instantly struck a chord was a fishing scene, depicting two groups of men on a sea shore, hauling in a net that had been cast just off the beach. Only six months earlier we had filmed exactly the same scene at sunrise on a beach in Spain; this method of catching large quantities of tiny fish from the shoreline had remained unaltered for thousands of years.

Once Ali and co. had cleared us to film an ancient site, we were often left to our own devices, but then keeping the tourists out of shot meant someone from the crew embarking on a tricky piece of PR. This was usually our sound recordist, George, who had just the right amount of tact and authority.

As most of the film was going to be dubbed over with commentary, there was not a lot of 'live' sound to be recorded. So once he had done a couple of 'atmos' tracks (general background sound of a location), George was free to help us in other areas. He seemed to revel in the challenge.

If a parked car needed moving, an official placating or a group of tourists held back for a couple of minutes, George would be dispatched to solve the problem. Having gone to 'a good school' he was able to turn on a mixture of charm and assertiveness that worked wonders, even with people who spoke hardly a word of English but seemed to respond to that touch of Officer Training Corps that underlay George's PR skills (George always claimed that he had avoided OTC at school but the rest of us had our suspicions). I'm sure if we'd asked him to have the pyramids moved slightly to one side he'd have happily trotted off to have a word with some chap.

After four days we moved out of Cairo and headed north towards Alexandria. The main impression on entering the countryside was that little had changed since biblical times.

Irrigation wheels were still driven by blindfolded cattle; elsewhere donkeys provided the main form of both transport and agricultural power. Colourful roadside markets were crowded with women, their shopping inside large baskets balanced on their heads with effortless grace. Just try that the next time you're in Tesco's.

We spent a day in the cotton fields with girls who seemed to have been flown in from top model agencies around the world, and by eleven o'clock I'd fallen in love seventeen times. For a day's labour they received the princely sum of seventy five pence, yet they could have earned a fortune doing the magazine covers of Paris and New York. Must be all that healthy outdoor living and simple life.

In Alexandria we acquired seven, and then a record eight, government minders, all of whom insisted on accompanying us on our trip around the port and to one of the newly constructed sea walls. Even with Ali fighting our cause, the bureaucratic hassles of getting filming clearance were now dragging on until midday. I began to suspect an ulterior motive, as the officials were always keen to partake of an ample lunch at our expense. The word was obviously getting around that there is such a thing as a free lunch.

The location after Alex was the small fishing port of El Burg, on the shores of both the Med and the inland Lake Burullus. With a slimline entourage of just five minders, we drove to the port to find it in the grip of a military operation. The main street was lined with six trucks of soldiers, whose presence could only mean something serious: a military exercise, civil uprising or an imminent threat of invasion. After all the fuss over filming churches and bridges I couldn't understand why we were being allowed within fifty miles of what was obviously a sensitive military area.

We eventually discovered that the cause of Operation Brave Defender was nothing more than a little old lady. She had apparently committed the heinous crime of living in a small house that had been built on the sea shore without planning permission. Shock horror. The authorities' action was swift and dramatic. On our return one hour later the house had been completely demolished and Granny placed under arrest. At that very moment she was probably bouncing around in the back of an army truck surrounded by swarthy Egyptian squaddies. So maybe think twice next time you start getting stroppy with the planning office over that extension to the patio.

We spent the afternoon on a felucca, a small local fishing smack. Unfortunately our craft had no joy catching anything, so we sailed back to port to await the return of a more successful vessel. By the time a boat with a catch arrived, we had attracted a large crowd and found ourselves trying to film in the middle of an Egyptian rugby scrum. Our minders then started giving us a hard time, because the fish were being landed next to a fly-infested house where apparently a young boy lay dying, not an image of modern Egypt the authorities were keen to present. I think we managed to grab a few shots of the fish being unloaded, but the main feature of the afternoon was yet another stormy argument between Geoff and the Powers That Be.

We completed our filming on the coast and headed back towards Giza, where we visited the museum that lies in the shadow of the Cheops pyramid. The museum houses a long wooden barge, discovered in 1954, buried deep in a pit next to the pyramid. The barge was supposed to transport Cheops to the next world, but oddly enough was not fully constructed but laid out in kit form. Perhaps Cheops was a keen modeller and was looking for some way to pass the time on his journey to the Other World.

Although over 4,000 years old, the boat's cedar timbers were perfectly preserved, encased in an airtight tomb of limestone blocks and mortar. Modern science, however, had not been able to match ancient technology. The Swedish-built museum had been unable to create the right atmospheric climate and after only thirty years the wood started to show signs of deterioration. Makes you wonder how they ever managed to build a Volvo.

Our final day in Egypt was spent on the Suez Canal, scene of numerous past conflicts. At one point the canal had been closed to ships by vessels sunk to block the hundred-mile passageway from the Gulf of Suez to the Mediterranean.

We were due to rendezvous with a tanker passing through the canal, but this was far from straightforward as the vessel was not able to stop and pick us up on the way. So we had to charter a small motorboat, come alongside the tanker and then make several trips to take the equipment up the viciously steep gangway to the deck some five storeys above us. Once on board we had to complete the filming and then make the return trip back to our boat, all within the thirty-minute window that the tanker captain had allowed us.

In our manic attempts to beat the clock we collided frequently on the narrow gangway but managed to get off the ship with seconds to spare. Back on the canal bank we piled into the van and sped down the highway to overtake the ship for a final shot of the huge tanker sailing through the sand. Wha'dya mean they did that in *Lawrence of Arabia*?

By the time of our departure I was more than ready to return to England, having spent most of the previous nine months travelling around Spain, France, Greece, Turkey and Egypt, with an interim trip to Japan, America, France again and Germany. During that time I'd experienced just about every form of transport known to man: jumbo jet, light aircraft, helicopter, coach, minibus, car, truck, train, hovercraft, hydrofoil, tanker, yacht, powerboat, motorboat, trawler, fishing smack, rowing boat - and donkey.

And the film they showed on the flight back to London? *Planes, Trains and Automobiles.*

Winging the world with Whicker

I once read an interview with a film producer who said that one attraction of working freelance was that your life could change with a single telephone call. A trifle melodramatic perhaps, but as I was living in Elephant and Castle at the time it wouldn't have taken much of a phone call to significantly alter my life.

One such call did occur - about a job for British Telecom. They wanted a series of corporate videos, purely for BT staff, to demonstrate how well the company was doing worldwide.

The project involved travelling to Japan, America, France and Germany, comparing BT with the hottest of the white-hot technological nations, the home of 'Ma Bell' (AT&T) and the best that Europe had to offer. The tight schedule dictated that this was going to be no cruisy jaunt around the world but more of a whistle-stop tour, with only a few days in each location while laughing in the face of jet-lag.

On such a trip, trying to keep track of hours worked, travel-time, breaks and the like is a mathematical nightmare, so the crew agreed a flat rate for the job to compensate us for being on call at all times. When it came to hammering out a deal, Catherine, the producer, proved a tough negotiator.

'If you don't come on this all-expenses-paid First Class trip around the world, we won't give you lots of money.'

Oh, alright then.

An added bonus was the chance to work with Alan Whicker, who was going to be presenting the series. It's always slightly unnerving meeting someone whom you have watched on television since childhood, but I was looking forward to him playing the bon viveur over dinner, recounting tales of the rich and famous. It would also give me a chance to brush up my Pythonesque impersonation.

So I was flattered when he came over to introduce himself on the first day - and that was the last time he spoke to me. I must have made a great impression.

In fact none of us ever got to know the man behind the image, and this turned out to be the only disappointment of the trip. A consummate professional, he was always pleasant and polite but somewhat distant, veering away from mixing with the crew, even though there were just six of us. Admittedly logistics sometimes prevented us from eating or travelling together, but there were plenty of other opportunities to socialise.

That said, we each received a copy of his autobiography at the end of the job. It was only on reading it later that I began to understand his detached view towards mixing with the troops. His early career in the fifties and sixties was spent covering long, arduous and often dangerous assignments, sometimes with a crew of just himself and the cameraman. By the seventies, however, the trade union was insisting on large crews and working practices that Whicker must have thought ludicrous in the light of his early experience. Consequently he seemed to regard all film crews as underworked union fanatics, and so preferred to keep his distance.

Since the demise of union power in the eighties, crew numbers have reduced dramatically and technicians have had to become more flexible about the scope of their jobs. So I felt that Whicker may have been tarring us with a very old brush.

Nevertheless we still drink beer and say 'fuck' a lot.

Having done most of my flying with 'the bucket and spade brigade' (the cabin crew's term for economy passengers), travelling British Airways First Class to Tokyo was total self-indulgence: attendants oozing charm, cuisine to bring tears to the palate and seats that welcomed you with a loving embrace. All conspired to create the atmosphere of an exclusive London club at 37,000 feet. It's difficult to hang on to socialist principles while being thoroughly doused in elitist luxury - but come The Revolution, everyone will fly First Class.

Tokyo was an eye-opener, useful when you're jet-lagged after a thirteen-hour flight. It has all the ingredients necessary for an urban disaster: overcrowding, cramped housing and an ugly sprawl of double-decker motorways and office blocks that does little to please the eye. Yet it maintains a sense of order and propriety that is lacking in any Western city. There may be major crime, such as corporate fraud, and serious criminals, like the *Yakuza* (the Japanese Mafia), but there is virtually no street crime i.e. no graffiti, vandalism, mugging or rape. In public at least, the Japanese sense of discipline and respect for authority prevails.

Hence a pedestrian waiting patiently for the 'Cross' sign at a deserted minor junction on a quiet Sunday morning. Hence one million pristine vending machines throughout the city, selling not only chocolate and cigarettes but also beer, whisky and - incredibly - jewellery. Hence the relief of our producer who, having left her wallet in a phone box, returned some time later to find it untouched.

The seed for this strict social order seem to be sown at the earliest age. From the start, kids are drilled to work hard and have respect for others. School hours are from eight till six, Monday to Friday. Secondary school children studying for university entrance attend evening cramming classes, getting home at about eleven, and *then* starting homework set by both day school and night class. Hence the expression, 'pass with four, fail with five', referring to the number of hours' sleep one should have while studying.

On leaving school the work ethic continues unabated. It's fundamental to Japanese class structure, as a person's position on the corporate ladder determines their place in society. A managerial job is usually for life, even if one ends up being moved discreetly sideways to become a 'window manager' i.e. you are given a desk near a window and attend meetings, but your job is fairly meaningless.

In return companies expect and largely receive unswerving devotion. Executives can work six, sometimes seven days a week, including evenings, and rarely take all their holidays. Inevitably some managers end up collapsing (and sometimes dying) through exhaustion, a phenomenon known as *karoshi*.

We checked into our hotel in central Tokyo. Our local contact, Buddy, and his two assistants marshalled an army of porters who descended on our luggage in a frenzy. With much commotion and bowing, the cases were swiftly tagged and whisked off to our rooms.

Japanese customer service is a wonder to behold. In my room, I inadvertently let the door swing shut behind me with the key still in the outside lock. A few seconds later a knock at the door revealed a bowing, smiling and kimonoed chambermaid, proffering the key in upturned palms as if it was a lotus blossom. I thanked her and bowed in acceptance. She bowed back, only slightly lower. I bowed again and started to shut the door, but she wasn't having it. We continued bowing through the closing door like two nodding dogs.

You see this courtesy and etiquette everywhere. Businessmen meeting each other present their cards with upturned palms, details facing the receiver. This allows both parties to instantly assess their respective status and determine the bowing regime that will follow a split second later. Hence a senior executive might offer just a slight tilt of the head, while a junior manager would end up face-first in the Axminster.

Similarly, attendants on an inter-city train would never leave the carriage without first turning to the passengers to bow and offer a small speech of thanks. Can you really see that happening on one of Richard Branson's trains? And watching a group of middle-class, middle-aged women in kimonos greet each other in the hotel foyer was to observe a display of pure charm.

A new experience for me was also the complete lack of tipping. In a country where so much status is attached to one's job, offering a tip is deemed to be deeply insulting, as it implies that the 'tippee' has an occupation of little value or worth. Must try that next time I take a cab in London.

'I have no wish to offend your honourable profession by demeaning you with a gratuity.'

'I'm much obliged, guv.'

At the first production meeting Buddy handed out our four-day schedule. The days seemed to be divided into periods of ten minutes with nonstop filming from dawn to dusk. Somehow he'd managed to cram fourteen hours into Wednesday morning. Thursday was going to be a cracker. You could tell it was going to be a bit special from Buddy's scripted legend at the top of the page: 'Big Day Thursday - let's get yourselves together'.

Day One was spent dashing around central Tokyo, interviewing expat BT workers and filming the dealing floor of one of the largest securities companies. Telecom had managed to beat off the domestic competition to supply all the dealing screens and communications systems (in Japanese!), a real achievement given the excellence of the domestic suppliers.

The Big Day Thursday arrived and we all got ourselves together. We were travelling by train to the southern city of Kyoto to film the ancient temples and surrounding district. We went on the famous Bullet Train, introduced in the sixties as the fastest passenger train in the world and also the first to feature an on-board public payphone.

The Japanese train system excels beyond belief. You know it's different the moment you walk onto the platform and see the station guards in their immaculate uniforms, all gleaming buttons and glaringly white gloves. All along the edge of the platform is a series of numbers. These refer to the carriages; your carriage number is on your ticket. When the train pulls in, the door of your carriage will stop, to the inch, at its position marked on the platform.

The Japanese system holds a further jewel: if any inter-city train is more than five minutes late both the driver and guard are fined (!) and the passengers receive a refund (!!) On that basis I reckon both Richard Branson and old BR owe me several thousand in back pay (but then in Japan you wouldn't get announcements as priceless as this one from a

BR guard, 'British Rail wish to announce that due to unforeseen circumstances this train will be arriving on time....')

As we approached Kyoto we were warned that the strict adherence to timetables meant that the train would remain at the station for two minutes and two minutes only. For the average traveller this wouldn't be a problem, but we had fifteen cases of equipment to get through the narrow corridor. Getting us and all the gear off in time promised a challenging arrival in Kyoto.

Our electrician, Nick, hit the platform running and was collecting cases before the train came to a halt. Mike (camera), Chris (sound) and myself formed a chain as Julie (our production manager) shouted out countdown times from the platform. The last case was out after forty-two seconds. The station's commuters, carrying nothing more than the regulation black attaché cases, looked as shocked as Japanese regulations would permit.

Kyoto is some 270 miles southeast of Tokyo and for nearly a thousand years until the middle of the last century was the capital of Japan. Today it is still very much the centre of culture and Buddhism, boasting the Imperial Palace and an incredible array of Buddhist temples and Shinto shrines.

Yet amid all this tradition, modern communication thrives with an array of phone booths. BT-style boxes stood alongside Japanese versions of the old red British model, while tradition was honoured with a box in the style of an ancient temple.

This contrast of ancient and modern provided a wide range of material for our film, keeping us as busy as Buddy's schedule had promised. By the time we arrived back in Tokyo, the day had turned into one of those sixteen-hour specials that are typical of the filming business.

Nine a.m., Friday morning, the Emperor's Palace Gardens. Tried to be blasé about filming in one of the world's most exclusive locations but failed miserably. The Gardens are only open to the public on the Emperor's birthday, yet we had managed to gain access outside that hallowed anniversary. And if you are a devotee of meaningless statistics, then here's a humdinger: property prices in central Tokyo are so high that instead of trying to estimate the value of the Gardens as the ultimate piece of prime real estate ('handy for the city'), it is simply priced on a par with the State of California.... The mind boggles at the thought of negotiating that purchase deal: 'I'm sorry I can't go any higher than Texas.'

The Gardens provided a stunning backdrop to a walk'n'talk interview with BT's head honcho in Tokyo, an expat who extolled the way Japanese business combines a brash 'can-do-and-let's-do-it-now' attitude with traditional courtesy and etiquette.

On our last day in Tokyo we visited an exclusive and expensive tea house, a sanctuary from the hustle of the outside world. Yet even here a telephone was at hand, albeit discreetly hidden under an ornate silk square. We didn't stay for the whole ceremony as it can last several hours, a world away from, 'stick the kettle on luv and make us a cuppa'.

The filming complete, we packed up in preparation for Los Angeles. The whirlwind trip had provided a glimpse into the style and spirit of modern-day Japan. The pressures on Tokyo's citizens are such that in any country other than Japan, the city would be in flames. After such a brief visit I couldn't say how or why tradition and respect could survive such urban congestion, but I envied them for it. As we drove to the airport, I fantasised about a London with no graffiti, litter, theft, vandalism, mugging or rape - and immaculate telephone boxes.

We left the Land of the Rising Sun, where tipping is regarded as an insult, and travelled to the Land of the Sinking Smog, where failing to tip someone is a calculable health risk. There can be few cities more inappropriately named than the 'City of the Angels'.

We negotiated Customs and Immigration without too many difficulties. I was slightly disappointed at not being asked if I was now or ever had been a member of the Communist Party (I haven't, but it would have been nice to have been asked). They'd also dropped the question on the immigration form about whether I was intending to overthrow the Government of the United States - 'Sole purpose of visit....'

Outside the airport terminal we met our two drivers, Chuck and Rick (who else?), a couple of Totally Awesome Bodacious Dudes who, given the scale of film-making in Los Angeles, must have regarded our measly kit as suitable for little more than home movies.

As we began loading the cases into the camera van, we were approached by a police officer who looked as if he spent his weekends playing Defence (or "De-fense") for the LA Raiders.

'Would you like to move this ve-hickle or would you like to make a contribution to the Los Angeles Police Department?' he drawled.

Hey, this guy was good, straight from Central Casting (Category: wisecracking Law Enforcement Officer; tough but fair; very large).

I resisted the temptation to ask him what the going rate was for parking bribes, and assumed he was referring to the fine that was approaching at a rate of knots. We quickly packed up the van and moved off. Welcome to LA and, hey - have a nice day.

Whicker was staying at the Beverley Hills Hotel, which with its ostentatious opulence and rich pageant of movie star guests, I'd imagined to be the top place in town. Wrong. The Beverley Hills is the place where the garishly famous go to be seen - but the lesser-known Sunset Marquis, just south of Sunset Boulevard, is where the discerningly famous (Bruce Springsteen, Phil Collins) go not to be seen - and that's where we were staying. A low profile two-storey building set back from a quiet sidestreet, the only clue to its existence was a discreet awning over the entrance to an underground car park.

Inside was an oasis of cool, calm and quiet charm. I looked around in awe. It was some way on from my days as an impoverished student at Bristol Old Vic Theatre School and the freezing £5-a-week tiny bedsit I'd endured for a year.

After unpacking, the production team went off to slum it by the pool while the director, Mike and myself decided that jet lag was for wimps and went off to grab some general shots of the city.

Until you've seen advertising hoardings in LA, you ain't seen nuthin', dudes. A fifty-foot high Marlboro' Man cowboy extols the virtues of shortening your life by handy seven-minute segments. Bruce Willis stares down at you from a height to which even his ego could not aspire. And Dirty Harry's Magnum could have doubled for one of the guns of Navarone.

That evening we went out for dinner and took advantage of the hotel's courtesy car, one of the ridiculous stretch limos that are *de rigueur* for LA society. Cruising in such a vehicle was probably a first for all of us, as we played with the toys on offer (TV, stereo, car phone, cocktail cabinet) like excited kids on Christmas Day morning. Needless to say, not all back-seat limo activity is this innocent. Our driver told us tales of limos halting at traffic lights, at which point items of underwear would come flying out of the windows.

The following day we started filming at Muscle Beach, where I felt distinctly out of place. The 'bods', waddling ads for steroid abuse, work out in what must be the most antiquated gym in America. But given its open-air locale next to the babe-packed beach, it's perfect for serious posing. We attracted a few stares from passers-by not, I suspect, because we were a film crew (who are ten a penny over there) but more for our unconventional appearance i.e. we weren't roller skating in pink leotards with a python draped around our necks.

Along the promenade we interviewed a local telephone company employee, who explained the many facets and unexpected limitations of America's phone system. While private phones can have facilities akin to a small exchange, public phones are surprisingly restrictive. Unless you own a credit card, all calls have to be made by cash, as apparently Americans can't handle the notion of a phonecard, or indeed anything where you have to pay for something before you use it.

Furthermore, payphones will only accept small coins, maximum 25 cents, so to make a call you first have to visit McDonalds and buy a large shake, thus acquiring a container big enough for all the coins you'll need. And with the break-up of AT&T ('Ma Bell') into several independent companies (the 'Baby Bells'), different aspects of the phone system are now handled by different companies. So you have one account for the actual phone, another for local calls and a third for long-distance calls. And long-distance calls can involve more than one operator to access the lines of different companies across the country. It all made even the telephone days of the Post Office seem a model of efficiency.

We spent the next day cruising up and down Sunset Boulevard on the back of one of the special film tracking vehicles that are used to provide a stable platform for moving shots. With dampened suspension and a variety of camera mounts including a small crane, the tracking vehicle can offer a range of options for filming at speed.

The version we used resembled a very low-level car transporter, which in effect is what it was. Any close-up shots of a travelling car are taken by first driving the car on to the ramp which sits some six inches above the road, and then positioning the camera as desired anywhere on the walkway around the vehicle. This explains those head-on car interior shots where you see an actor apparently moving the steering wheel from side to side while the car proceeds serenely along a perfectly straight road.

Not that it needed it, but the film *Pretty Woman* gave worldwide exposure to Rodeo Drive, the ultimate shopping precinct in this Mecca of born-to-shop acolytes. The stratospheric level of consumerism that abounds along this avenue of avarice is such that it is deemed the height of bad manners to ask the price of an item (and if you have to ask, you probably can't afford it). Certain shops receive customers solely by appointment. Somehow I can't see this ever catching on at Woolies.

We were hoping to film on the Drive to catch some of the city's beautiful people, although on the day we were there we could find only their stand-ins. Filming on a busy street is always fraught with difficulties (gear security, clear sightlines, blocking the footpath), but when that street happens to be the most exclusive shopping zone in the world, problems of a different nature arise.

Wherever you film in LA you need a permit which, given the number of productions at any one time, ensures that the city doesn't get overrun by film crews taking over busy streets. But the permit system is also, as Arthur Daley would put it, 'a nice little earner'. If you want to film anywhere within the city limits, you pay, and the more prestigious the location the higher the rate. Hence you can imagine the cost of trying to film on Rodeo Drive. So-o-o.... we winged it.

Our local fixer, Barbara, seemed fairly nonchalant about breaking the city's regulations.

'If anyone asks, tell them you're part of the production filming down the road.' A *bona fide* and no doubt permitted crew had sealed off a section of a nearby street.

My suspicion that this all seemed a bit too relaxed was confirmed when it transpired that only Mike and I would actually be out there in the firing line, should the police question us. Barbara and our director were going to be discreetly absent during our illegal activities. The phrase 'cannon fodder' came to mind.

We walked onto Rodeo Drive as casually as possible. Mike set up the sticks (tripod) and camera, while I strolled up the street to look out for any approaching black-and-whites containing LA's finest.

Everything was going smoothly when suddenly a police car appeared at the top of the street. Some fifty yards away from Mike, I could hardly cry out, 'Mike! Look out! The cops!' But he resolutely refused to see my surreptitious attempts at frantic waving. I started back towards him, but without breaking into an attention-grabbing run I knew there was no way I could warn him in time. The police car cruised past me.

I was contemplating the film crew equivalent of name, rank and serial number as the car drew slowly level with Mike. The driver eyeballed him curiously.... before continuing down the street.

'Thanks for the warning,' said Mike accusingly.

'Well, I waved,' I replied defensively. 'You try waving surreptitiously.'

Perhaps they had bigger fish to fry, but the next two police cars also glided by without stopping. Now if Clint had been on duty, it might have been a different matter....

After five days we flew out of LA and headed towards New York. For all of LA's reputation as the holy city in the land of milk and honey, it was not somewhere that I would ever choose to live. Sure the smog's bad, but when you've been brought up among the coal pits of northeast England (cue Hovis ad), it pales by comparison. Essentially LA seemed a very superficial place, with neither spiritual nor physical heart (the city has no actual centre but is simply a sprawling grid of blocks and districts).

I reckon the old joke about a pot of yoghurt having more culture than LA sums it up pretty neatly.

New York has to be the least disappointing city in the world. Yep, it's rude, brash, loud and aggressive - 'Excuse me officer, can you tell me the way to Times Square or should I go screw myself?' - but it's *supposed* to be like that. What you see on the movies is what you get on the street. I can think of no other city in the world where that can be stated with such conviction.

Our local contact was a laid-back dude called Sander, a Springsteen clone from 'Noo Joisey' with every one of Bruce's songs etched in the lines on his face. On seeing the

Manhattan skyline for the first time as we drove over the Brooklyn Bridge, I let out a very uncool 'Wow!' Sander gave me what I can only describe as an old-fashioned look.

It may be the ultimate cliché shot, but I defy anyone to film in New York without including at least one vista of that incredible skyline. I know every major city has its tall buildings, but it's only when you see them crammed together in neck-stretching phalanxes that you appreciate how unique the place is. The older skyscrapers in particular, such as the Woolworth and Chrysler buildings, built before the days of the soulless glass towers, are as wondrous structures as any of the world's cathedrals. They may be monuments to Mammon, but perhaps God doesn't have all the best architects.

Most of our time was spent on Wall Street, interviewing various high-powered executives about British Telecom and the state of the competition. In a city where any exposed jugular is fair game, BT's success could be judged from the fact that the securities company, Merrill Lynch, whose trading floor with some 1200 screens is possibly the largest in the world, had chosen BT equipment for their dealing network. As Whicker would say, on the Boulevard of Bucks BT was moving the money and making merry in Manhattan.

I realise how much I've been influenced by working with Whicker. I keep amassing assorted assemblages of assonant alliteration: avenue of avarice, monuments to Mammon, Boulevard of Bucks, moving the money.... It has become his trademark and quite often during the project Alan would take the script as provided by BT and blatantly 'Whickerise' it. He almost seemed to be parodying Monty Python's brilliant tribute to him: 'Here in this colonial Campari land, waterfalls of whisky wash away the worries of a world-weary Whicker....'

He was fascinating to watch during an interview. Any nerves on the part of the interviewee would soon melt away in the face of his old-world charm, yet often when the interview was over and the subject departed, he could be coldly dismissive of them. Then when we did the reverse shots of Alan for his questions (needed to edit the interview) he would switch on the charm and sincere interest again, even though he was now performing to no-one. His noddies (reaction shots where he nods in apparent agreement with the interviewee) were superb, feigning sympathy, empathy, interest and laughter as appropriate. What a pro.

He usually got his pieces-to-camera right on the first take and we had to be on our toes, as any request to go again for camera or sound was not well received.

On our final day we travelled to Liberty State Park on the shores of New Jersey to illustrate an example of the absurd irrationality that the US payphone system can present. Just a mile across the Hudson River stood the twin towers of the World Trade Centre, yet incredibly a call to the restaurant on top of one of the towers was 'long distance' and charged accordingly. We never did understand the toll call system but it made Britain's integrated network seem a haven of sanity.

The residents of the Big Apple seem to have a love-hate relationship with their city. Wherever you go you hear people venting their frustrations with the phrase, 'Only in Noo Yawk....' This is trotted out so often that it has become as much a cliché as those rather cutesy bumper stickers declaring 'I (heart) NY'. Personally I'd never live there in a million years, but I can appreciate the seductive challenge of life in the fast lane and to hell with the speed limit. Yes, it's everything that's horrendous about big city living, but it must be immensely satisfying to know, as the man said, that if you can make it there, then you can probably make it anywhere.

Paris has always been one of my favourite cities, for the simple reason that you don't really have to do anything to have a good time. It is a city of simple pleasures, of walking down splendid boulevards, sipping coffee in sidewalk cafes and watching the world's most beautiful women cruise serenely by.

For all of France's fierce pride in everything French and the volatile history of Anglo-French relations, they are not averse to buying British when it suits them. Hence Air France, a flagship company in a flag-waving country, had opted for BT equipment in preference to a domestic system.

Under the strictest security conditions, we were allowed a brief stint in their air traffic control centre, although most of our attempts to film the high-tech equipment there were met by a resounding 'Non!' They'd probably have said the same had we tried to film the canteen microwave.

After Paris we flew to Frankfurt. Given the Germans' reputation for order and discipline, we had expected a well-run society with few of the problems that seem to plague British cities. However we found Frankfurt a rather dull and grey place with a depressing attitude to everyday life, allied to a surprising amount of vandalism, particularly to the city's telephone boxes.

Nevertheless, the cobblestone square in the heart of old Frankfurt provides a classic chocolate-box image. In one of the cafes we indulged in some life-shortening gateaux before interviewing another of BT's expat ambassadors. He revealed that despite *Vorsprung durch Technik,* the German phone system paled against a bit of BT boffinry.

With our journey now complete, we celebrated with a memorable night in one of the city's many bierkeller. Actually it wasn't that memorable as the details are still a little hazy, but the following day I was assured by the crew that I had given a stirring, full-volume rendition of *Born In The USA*, much to the consternation of the local patrons.

'Zis Bruce Springsteen - he is looking much taller on ze videos....'

At the end of the job I came away with a changed attitude to BT. I had been as intolerant of their past sins as most people, but was now genuinely impressed by their world standing. The trip also turned me into something of a phone-spotter. I've always had a fear of developing an interest in things mundane (I call it anoraknaphobia), but I realise I've acquired an unhealthy knowledge of phone boxes round the world and can speak about them with authority for several minutes. This is a product of documentary film- making: by temporarily immersing yourself in a variety of subjects, you end up being superficially knowledgeable on a range of esoteric topics.

There were plans for additional trips to the Middle East, Australasia and South America but then an item appeared in the *Daily Mail*, exposing our trip and castigating BT for having spent so much money on such an apparently frivolous project. Yea, ever seen a journalist's expenses claim? I'm not sure whether the article was responsible, but shortly afterwards there was a change in BT management and the planned trips were all cancelled.

Nevertheless it had been an amazing job, a glimpse into the seemingly limitless possibilities of information technology and providing experiences and memories that have remained vivid to this day. Now if only that phone would ring again....

You're being paid to go to the Bahamas?!!

When I was first struggling to get into the industry, I would hear about crews swanning off to the Caribbean on what seemed to be the ultimate job: being paid to go and do something you enjoy in a location that is definitely in the dream holiday category. So I was ready for the spluttering reaction on telling people that I was about to go off to Nassau in the Bahamas to film a commercial for a Caribbean rum. 'You're being paid?' I tried not to gloat but failed miserably.

At the time I was working in New Zealand, which teetering as it does on the edge of the earth, seems about as far away as you can get from wherever you want to go. Consequently the journey to Nassau took thirty-six hours, complete with twelve cases of gear and three changes of plane. Having left Auckland in the evening, by the time I reached Nassau I was entering my third day without proper sleep and so was a touch ragged at the edges.

Then I lost my passport.

We were due to start filming immediately and having been warned of the local pickpockets I had decided to leave my passport in the hotel room. The best my sleep-deprived brain could come up with was to hide the document under the mattress (how original). One hour later I'd completely forgotten that I'd ever hidden it. The ensuing search took two hours and involved a fruitless trip back to the airport, convinced that I'd left it at the customs on arrival. Strange what a lack of sleep can do.

Eventually the cerebral mists cleared and I had a sudden flashback. With an extravagant gesture that would have done credit to a legion of hotel-wrecking rock-stars I threw aside my mattress, revealing the treasured item. It felt like days since I'd left it there.

On telling the rest of the crew, they subjected me to the inevitable verbal abuse. But at least I wasn't going to be stuck in the Bahamas, with all those beaches, sparkling waters, endless days of sunshine. Hang on a minute....

We began filming in the local markets of downtown Nassau. As soon as we started, we knew we had struck gold. The images were manna from heaven: bright colours, beaming smiles and a parade of local street life.

Generally when out among the public, a film crew attracts a certain amount of attention, usually just good-natured curiosity, but you are always aware of your sore-thumb profile. Oddly enough, this didn't seem to apply to us. People would wander past with barely a glance, making our task of capturing life in the market much easier.

We discovered this nonchalance was born out of seen-it-all-before indifference. They'd had film crews from every type of production, from holiday programmes to the full-blown spectacle of the James Bond films. No problem, man. And with that background came a street-wise savvy when it came to being asked to appear on camera. However, one islander's natural exuberance got the better of his business acumen.

'Would you mind being on camera for us?'

'It'll cost you fifty dollars, man.'

'We'll give you five.'

'A'right - and I'll sing a song.'

We also came across the next middleweight boxing champion of the world - or so he professed. Frank was doing what appeared to be a fairly casual work-out on the beach when we turned up for some general shots. Obviously one of life's characters, he was a must for the camera, although he was very specific as to what we could and could not film.

'Don't shoot me feet, man,'cos they're me secret weapon. If any of me opponents saw me footwork in training, they'd be ready for me in the ring.'

We managed to shoot some scenes without giving away Frank's master plan for the domination of world boxing. He certainly seemed to have the dedication required to make it to the top, as he told us his rigid lifestyle forbad any alcohol or female company. The shots completed, we thanked Frank and gave him the agreed appearance fee.

'Ah, great man - now I can take me girlfriend out for a drink tonight.'

We continued filming around the island, capturing glimpses of its carefree lifestyle: lazy beach bars, jet skiers bouncing over the surf and kids playing pool at a roadside café. The seductive palm trees around the café presented a rare but real danger I'd never experienced before - falling coconuts. Still, I guess it's one of the more exotic means of meeting one's fate - but you'd know that everyone at your funeral would be sniggering.

If you've seen the seventies thriller *Don't Look Now*, you'll remember the theme of a small figure in red that is fleetingly glimpsed several times, but never fully encountered until the film's climax. During our first day in the markets we came across the motoring equivalent of that figure: a bright pink Cadillac.

We were facing away from the street taking close-ups of one of the stores when the Cadillac cruised by behind our backs. Not only was it bright pink, it also bore the legend 'Return of the Pink Panther', with the cartoon panther lounging lazily down one side. Kerry, the director, did a fair impersonation of the head-turning scene from *The Exorcist* and dashed off in fruitless pursuit as the vehicle swept away.

He returned disconsolate, but with a passionate gleam in his eye.

'We've *got* to get that on film!'

'Isn't that Elvis over there?'

'I'm not interested.'

From that moment on the Cadillac seemed to taunt us, appearing fleetingly at the end of a street or someway off in the distance, but always just out of shot and never long enough for us to whip the camera around and grab a few frames.

We tried to find out who owned the car but without success. Then, on our last morning, perhaps too obvious to have been considered, we discovered it was run by a local taxi company.

We quickly booked the car and spent the morning filming it. It had been used as a publicity vehicle for Peter Sellers during the filming of the *Return Of The Pink Panther*. The driver was also clad entirely in pink and called himself.... Pink. In the luxurious setting of the island it fitted in beautifully and was one of the highlights of the eventual commercial.

Over lunch I dashed off postcards to everyone I could think of - well, if you've got it, flaunt it, and I was probably never going to have this particular 'it' again. I began each card with 'Yawn, yawn, another day at the office....' Some people have never forgiven me.

Our last afternoon was spent filming some local samba dancers. We needed the backdrop of a brightly coloured wall and the best location turned out to be a local car park. Perhaps that more than anything else sums up the uniquely colourful nature of the island - after all, you could hardly imagine doing the same in an NCP in Dulwich.

Food, glorious food

'One of the less pleasant aspects of film-making with a British crew is that when you address them, the answers are usually muffled by mouthfuls of food.'

Thus moaned director John Boorman in his book *Money Into Light,* writing about the excesses of the catering on a major feature film. That said, a small-unit documentary crew can be lucky to grab a sandwich during a twelve-hour day, as real life proceeds regardless of meal breaks. One day Maxim's, next day McDonalds.

Food is vital to everyone, but on a big-budget production it often seems more important than the movie. Caterers are conjurors, with magic names such as *Reel Meals, Set Meals* or *The Wild Lunch.* They can produce sumptuous meals in the most taxing environments, so much so that I can be on my feet twelve hours a day lugging around camera cases and still put on weight.

The day begins with breakfast, which can be a gargantuan affair pandering to all tastes, from organic, free-range, liberal-thinking muesli to a traditional fry-up guaranteed to shorten your life by at least fifteen minutes.

Next is morning tea. If you indulge in nothing more than a biscuit and a cuppa then a film crew's mid-morning break would serve for most people's lunch: fruit, sandwiches, biscuits, muffins, plus several blends of teas, coffees, herbal teas, decaf coffee, coffee substitutes, hot chocolate, malt drinks, fruit juices and mineral water (sparkling or still).

OK, so you manage to stagger through to lunch, but if you're wilting now, you may as well go home.

To digress slightly, in recent times the midday meal has taken on a significance way beyond its humble function of fuelling the machine, and nowhere more than in the media industry. Advertising agency lunches are notorious for their excess. In the heady pre-crash days of the eighties, top agencies would compete to host the most outrageous, exorbitant lunches for their clients, the feasting sometimes continuing until two o'clock - the following morning. In Hollywood the power lunch has become an event, a status symbol and ultimately a weapon, with those who have offended the High Priests of Production being doomed to oblivion with the words, 'You'll never eat lunch in this town again!'

But back to the table. Ever sensitive to New Age demands, a top film catering company will cover all bases, so that no matter how fussy or finicky a crew, all their preferences will be met. The days when a vegetarian alternative to the 'main' meal was regarded as the ultimate in culinary liberalism are long gone. Vegan, herbivore, omnivore and probably cannibal are all catered for on request, while the traditional English Sunday roast can still be provided in the most inappropriate of settings: during the making of *The Killing Fields* roast beef and Yorkshire pudding appeared in the middle of the Thai countryside.

So you crawl back to work after a multi-course lunch and no sooner have you done one shot than afternoon tea arrives, with yet another array of cakes, biscuits, muffins, fruit, etcetera.

Thankfully that will usually be the last sustenance until you retire to the hotel for a well-deserved dinner - unless of course you are working late, in which case dinner and possibly even a late-night snack will have to be negotiated.

For the caterers, keeping a human machine of some seventy-plus components up and running in all weathers and locations requires a grasp of cunning and logistics that would defeat most military commanders. In the remotest locations, *cordon bleu* miracles appear en masse from the confines of a trailer or converted bus. Me, I can't cope with a dinner party for six in a fully equipped kitchen unless I get three days' notice.

Often their reputation extends beyond the confines of the set. While filming in Belfast we were guarded by the RUC, yet after a couple of days we noticed that our protection squad doubled around lunchtime. And the caterers' pride in their profession borders on the obsessive, which of course leaves them open to some merciless leg-pulling, as on one occasion when the grip produced a bread roll containing a prop rat.

''Ere, this roll's a bit off....'

When catering is not provided, the crew may be force-marched off to the nearest Michelin eatery. As a result I have eaten in some stunning restaurants around the world, courtesy of various production companies - thank you, one and all, particularly Thames Television, Third Eye Productions and September Films. But the most memorable meals have always been those served on set, proving the old adage that the best seasoning is a healthy appetite. If a crew has been up and running since before dawn, the only dish likely to cause instant loss of appetite is puree of fresh baby slug.

So, having drooled over culinary memories I suppose I'd better award my own Memorable Meals Medal. And the winner is.... the crew of the Spanish fishing trawler who we were filming as part of the *Encircled Sea* series about the Mediterranean. Breakfast was freshly caught sardines fried up on deck and washed down with a rough red wine poured from one of those vessels you hold two feet above your mouth. Lunch was a stunning fresh fish buffet, again served on deck with nothing but the empty horizon on all sides.

Maxim's, eat your heart out.

Singing for our supper

The vocal talents of opera star Dame Kiri Te Kanawa have been praised around the world for over two decades. Mine have not. (Although apparently give me an evening of several drinks and a loud-enough backing track and I can do a mean Springsteen.) But Maori tradition was to see me singing in public and in broad daylight, with neither accompaniment nor inebriation for support. Singing in public or root canal work? Too close to call.

The *South Bank Show*, London Weekend TV's arts programme, was doing a year-in-the-life documentary on Dame Kiri. After five years in the UK, she was returning home to New Zealand for the commemorations of the 1840 Treaty Of Waitangi, by which the British had claimed sovereignty over Maori lands. I was already working over there and was one of the five local crew hired by the visiting LWT producer.

We began with filming Kiri's open air concert in Wellington in front of 80,000 people and I found myself working directly in front of stage. The previous week I'd been just an ordinary spectator among the 150,000 who had seen her performance in Auckland. Then I was so far away it could have been Sly Stallone in the vivid pink dress. Now I was close enough to check her fillings.

The concerts completed, Kiri moved on to the more private aspects of her trip, which included a visit to her Maori tribe. She wasn't expected until midday but we planned to arrive in the morning, do some general shots and then film her formal entrance onto the *marae*, the tribal grounds.

Nigel, the producer, had discovered that Maori tradition required an exchange of songs between the elders of the tribe and the ourselves, the visiting 'tribe'. Film technicians are not renowned for their singing. Unaccompanied. In front of lots of people.

'What song have you chosen?' I enquired.

'Well, I wanted something well-known and appropriate for Kiri's visit.'

For one awful instant I thought it was going to be *There's No Business Like Show Business* and had visions of the whole crew doing an Ethel Merman.

'So we'll be singing *She'll Be Coming Round The Mountain*.'

The only version I knew of this was from *Rugby Songs III* - well known maybe, but hardly suitable for a returning diva. Fortunately the words had been modified for the occasion. A tame rendering of the song of my youth perhaps, but less likely to give offence than something akin to *Eskimo Nell*.

The two-hour drive to the location was spent rehearsing for what was to be both our opening and farewell concert. Despite our efforts, Nigel felt we lacked a certain passion ('You have to sell it, guys'), and proposed adding a few gestures to give our performance the necessary 'oomph' of a truly live event.

By the time we arrived we could have opened the Gang Show, although I'd persuaded Nigel to drop the clenched fist gesture, given that it might rekindle past Anglo-Maori hostilities. Impressed, he bowed to my superior knowledge of Maori custom (gleaned solely from watching the All Blacks perform their prematch *haka*).

The marae was a fenced-off grassy area of about an acre. It contained a graveyard and a small collection of single-level buildings, varying in size and design. Some were just modern huts but others more traditional, the most dominant being the large meeting house (*whare runanga*), built of wood, ornately carved and painted an earthy red.

Entering a marae involves a strict code of etiquette - and a challenge by a tattooed Maori warrior with a club-wielding display of martial arts. I'd seen these guys in action. They could stun your nose hair at ten paces.

We paused at the entrance as the warrior, wearing only the traditional flax skirt/kilt (*kinikini*), bounced forward in high-stepping style, the five-foot long club (*taiaha*) a blur of movement. A challenge was issued to see if we came in peace, ending with a single leaf being placed on the ground in front of us. As chief of our tribe, Nigel walked forward, picked up the leaf and stepped back without committing the grave offence of turning his back on the warrior. Having confirmed our peaceful intentions, we were in - nasal hair intact.

Once on the marae we took up our positions as guests. Then came an exchange of speeches. I'd mentioned to Nigel that Maori tradition regards rain on the first day of a venture as a good omen. Having already established my cultural credentials, he decided to include this in his opening address.

'We began our filming last week at Kiri's concert in Wellington and it rained....'

Pause for round of applause. A pin crashed to the ground. Good call, Hakin.

The speeches completed, the moment of truth arrived. Our small band of *pakeha* (the Maori term for the white European settlers) stood to address the assembled tribe. I steeled myself for what I suspected was going to be three minutes of bowel-moving embarrassment. Nigel bravely broke forth.

'She'll be coming round the mountain when she comes....'

The rest of us took up the strain. God knows what we sounded like, but whether out of pity or embarrassment, good-natured laughter broke out around the marae. Encouraged, we ploughed on, gestures and all, eventually reaching our grand finale. The end was greeted with stirring applause, probably out of relief that it was finally over. It is difficult for formality to remain after you have laid bare what little exists of your artistic soul, so we were able to relax and enjoy the considerable hospitality.

When Dame Kiri arrived she was welcomed home as a member of her tribe. Unlike us, she didn't have to sing for her supper but still gave a sublime rendition of an aria.

She didn't sound a lot like Springsteen either.

Touching lives

It hasn't all been beer and skittles. When making documentaries you are often invading someone's private and personal life, an experience that can be touching, enlightening or inspiring. The more serious side of the business has provided some of my strongest memories.

John lived in the small Scottish town of Galashiels. He had first began displaying symptoms of Tourette's Syndrome two years earlier when he was fourteen. Although a minor neurological disorder, Tourette's can manifest itself in spectacular fashion. Initially the effects on John were minimal, no more than rapid blinking, but as he got older the indications became more pronounced and dramatic. Now the illness had become a spasmodic display of spitting, loud yelps, sexual obscenities and involuntary punches, any one of which would occur about once a minute.

He spoke on two distinct levels, the normal everyday manner that betrayed no hint of his condition and sudden bursts of 'mind-speak', when he would inadvertently blurt out whatever he happened to be thinking at that moment. While anyone can have supplementary thoughts during a conversation, a filtering mechanism prevents us from verbalising those thoughts. John's condition however deprived him of that discretionary ability, and as an otherwise normal healthy sixteen-year-old boy, many of the exclamations were of a sexual nature.

He would try and stop these outbursts by suddenly biting his clenched fist, but no matter how quickly his hand flew to his mouth it was always that split second too late to prevent the emerging thought.

All this had a dramatic effect on John's life. Unable to walk through the town without attracting attention, he was often forced to make long detours when he ventured out. His physical spasms and loud yelps made him a mockery at school and caused problems with his teachers, while his

sexual outbursts upset many of his female classmates.
Consequently he was obliged to leave and attend special
lessons for slow learners at a local college, a cruel irony as
his intellect was clearly above average.

The effect on John's family was equally devastating. His
father simply chose to ignore the problem and kept out of the
way, indeed in the entire week we never saw him once.
John's grandmother regarded the illness as some form of
demonic possession (as the Church must have done in earlier
times) while his younger brother and sister, although
tolerating him to a point, clearly wished to have little to do
with him.

John's sole saviour was his mother, who perhaps because
of her training as a nurse seemed better equipped to deal
with the situation. Endlessly patient, she tolerated his
outbursts despite the often hurtful nature of the sexual
comments, and was there to help and guide as best she
could, such as when John's behaviour got him into trouble
with the local police.

On our first day I don't know who was more nervous,
John or us. He bounced into the lounge as we were setting
up the camera.

'Hullo baldy!' he announced to our follicly challenged
producer.

This was quite clearly going to be no ordinary week.

Nor were the rest of the crew spared John's observations.
Any physical feature was instantly pounced upon, and the
director and PA were made acutely aware of their female
gender. I managed to avoid being called Baldy, Big Nose or
Short Arse but was still regarded in a special light. John
watched intently as I loaded a magazine in the changing bag.

'I see, so you put the magazine and can of film into the
changing bag - *are you a poof?* - and then take the film out
of the can and place it in the magazine?'

'Er, yes, that's right,' I replied, not really sure what I was
affirming. When it came to (literally) speaking his mind,
John was probably the most honest person on the planet.

To illustrate the social problems that John faced, we filmed him in places that he normally would have avoided, such as the library, supermarket or walking down the high street. His behaviour drew a few glances, but I sensed that our own high profile made the passers-by generally ignore John's outbursts.

John's days at college seemed to place him under the most strain. Aware of the effects of his outbursts on others yet forced to mix in a social group, he felt that most people disliked him. At lunch times he would sit alone, eating his sandwiches in an empty classroom rather than face the hubbub of the college canteen.

Not that all was doom and gloom in his public life. Like many Touretters he was good at sports and excelled at basketball, where his high energies had a suitable outlet. Paradoxically the serenity of fishing on the local river also relieved John's condition, although his later admission that he avoided other anglers indicated that it was probably the solitude rather than the fishing that provided the calming influence.

As the week progressed, John became more relaxed around us while we became more accepting of his condition. Yet we still had to be on guard for his spontaneous punches. George, our sound recordist, was caught with a beaut of a left-hander when John unconsciously let fly, while I felt the rush of air when one flailing punch stopped just short of my face. As a boxer, John would have had the ultimate surprise punch, able to deliver it before even he knew anything about it.

By the end of the filming we had developed both a genuine liking for John and sympathy for his predicament. Given that Tourette's Syndrome is incurable, his options for dealing with it were pretty limited. Neurosurgery was not viable, the defect in his brain being so deep-seated and delicate that it would have been like trying to repair a microchip with a hammer. A psychiatric drug was available, but this would have had the effect of suppressing not only

the symptoms but his entire personality, leaving him to
wander around in a soporific stupor.

So he was left to live with his illness as best he could,
while also making the difficult transition from home and
special classes into adulthood and the outside world. How
much worse his condition would become it was impossible
to say, but he showed that he was still susceptible to new
facets of behaviour. During her research prior to our filming
Valerie, the director, had mentioned to John that at least he
did not spit, as did other Touretters.

'Oh, I'm glad I don't do that,' he replied, relieved. 'That
would be awful.' By the time we met him he had started
spitting.

Ultimately the real answer lay not with treating John but
helping those around him to understand and accept his
condition. It seemed the height of irony that John was
ostracised for swearing and making sexual remarks. Show
me a sixteen year-old who doesn't.

The programme was broadcast with the title *John's Not
Mad*. In a world that often seems so, John most certainly was
not.

To date my criminal record is pretty paltry, no more than a
couple of parking fines - ok, so there was that slight
misunderstanding over the Brinks Mat bullion job at
Heathrow, but as I was never formally arrested it seems a bit
picky to bring it up.

Nevertheless should I ever be tempted to try 'a bit of
business' I would only have to recall my brief sojourn in
Wandsworth prison to quell any deviant thoughts.

The arrival of AIDS into mainstream consciousness sent
the media into a feeding frenzy and I worked on a range of
programmes, the most memorable being a Government
information film for prison officers.

Due to the prevalence of both drug use and homosexual
behaviour, the rate of HIV infection among prisoners was far
higher than in the outside world. Given the potential for
violent disturbances within the prison, the Prison Officers

Association had become concerned that warders might contract HIV when dealing with any problems. So the Government commissioned a short film to reassure prison staff that because of the specific means of transmission, the chances of them contracting HIV were extremely low.

So off we go, five crew and six actors, for two days of porridge at the one-time temporary South London residence of one Ronald Biggs.

Wandsworth Prison is one of those evocative icons of the correctional system. Built in 1849, it can best be described as 'imposing'. The outside walls are high and stark, the inner buildings bleak and foreboding. None of your fancy Swedish penal hotel designs here. Lock 'em up and keep 'em in was presumably the brief brief given to the architect.

With no little sense of trepidation we marched through the prison to the clanging of doors and jangling of keys, reminiscent of *Porridge* and every gaol you've ever seen on the telly.

The film was to portray a range of situations representing the worst scenarios that a prison officer was likely to face. Each scene would then end with a doctor stating that, even in such extreme cases, you were unlikely to catch HIV.

Our location appeared to be the block for segregated prisoners, as each cell held just one person as opposed to the usual two or even three. Nevertheless even for a solitary prisoner, at ten feet by six the cells were a sobering place to spend twenty-three hours a day. Several prisoners hovered in the background on general cleaning duties, but otherwise the block was eerily quiet with no hint of the personalities behind each door.

The first scene was in the toilet area, all concrete, cold tiles and hard steel. It had some way to go to make the pages of *Ideal Bath and Bedroom*. The action concerned a young prisoner on his first day experiencing the delights of slopping out: each inmate empties his chamber pot into a what looks like a huge steel sink with a six-inch plughole, in effect a giant toilet bowl. A couple of veteran lags decide to initiate the newcomer and instigate a fight, during which the young prisoner is badly beaten and lies on the floor vomiting.

At this point a warder intervenes, and in the ensuing struggle has his hand bitten and the contents of a chamber pot thrown in his face before collapsing to the vomit-covered floor.

And you thought Monday mornings in the office were bad.

The props and make-up team of Jenny and Jez excelled themselves on the gory details. I don't know if they used diced carrots but the vomit was disgustingly realistic. The contents of the chamber pot defied description.

The actors playing the old lags were so well cast that I initially mistook one of them to be a real prisoner who had been called in as Technical Consultant. They took to their roles with gusto and although pulling their punches, made the scene sickeningly convincing. Then the prison officer waded in and tried to restore order, with all the messy consequences. Yet incredibly none of these events would be likely to transmit HIV, even if all of the prisoners concerned were HIV positive. Unbroken skin contact with infected blood and fluids is insufficient to contract the virus, nor will saliva entering a bite wound cause infection.

The scene for Day Two was inside one of the cells and re-created an unfortunately frequent event among segregated prisoners - attempted suicide. Given the strict control over what an inmate was allowed to have in his cell, there seemed no means of committing suicide, yet the ingenuity of someone in despair knows no bounds. One technique is to tear off strips of bedding, form them into a tourniquet around the neck, tie the other end to the pipes that run along the base of the wall and then repeatedly turn the body around to tighten the noose. Simple yet effective.

In keeping with the theory that suicide is more often a call for help than a genuine desire to die, some prisoners would literally stake their lives on the strict routine of prison life. Peephole inspection of cells took place at exactly the same times during the day, each inspection being reckoned to last a precise number of seconds. A prisoner wishing to make a convincing but unsuccessful suicide attempt would wait until the inspection began on the block, then commence his self-strangulation before hopefully being found in the nick of time.

The officer finding the prisoner would probably have to administer mouth-to-mouth resuscitation, and it was this intimate contact that was concerning the prison staff. So under the watchful eye of the real prison doctor we carefully bound our actor to the pipes, while Jenny applied the suitably blue pallor of someone at death's door. In our scene, the rescuing officer was able to revive the inmate. Again, as saliva contains such a tiny amount of the virus, there was no significant risk of transmission.

Our filming completed, we walked out of Wandsworth free men again, the sense of release palpable after a mere two days in the claustrophobic environment. Faced with two weeks, two months, two years in such a degrading atmosphere I would have grave doubts for my sanity. A visit to a prison and lecture from a long-serving con is often used to deter first-time offenders, but the idea could be extended to the general public. My two days inside Wandsworth were more than enough to keep me on the straight and narrow. And it would make a change from visiting the Tower.

The miners' strike of 84/85 was the most hard-fought industrial action of recent times. Mass picketing involved thousands on both sides, and in the heat of the moment law and order and civil liberties were often literally trampled underfoot. Many police were injured and many striking miners arrested. The story of one such miner brought an individual perspective to a dispute that was generally only seen on a grand scale.

It was an unusual job for me as I didn't come in until the end of the story. Our miner (whom we'll call Frank) had been arrested with several others while picketing at his local pit in Yorkshire. He claimed that in the heat of the moment the police had mounted a grab-and-snatch raid and simply arrested anyone they could get hold of.

Charged with throwing a petrol bomb, Frank was facing a possible jail sentence, yet as the trial approached the charge was repeatedly reduced, from throwing a petrol bomb to throwing a bottle, then a missile and eventually to an unspecified assault on a police officer. It didn't exactly add up to a solid charge.

I don't wish to appear biased or sentimental, but Frank was not one of the NUM's young bucks perhaps itching for a fight with the police. On the contrary, he seemed the very embodiment of a solid middle-aged family man. I could no more imagine him throwing a petrol bomb than my mother spying for the Russians (she didn't).

At his trial Frank was convicted of assault but given the unusual sentence of being forbidden for six months to go within fifty miles of his pit. As all his relatives lived in the area, this in effect kept him away from his entire family.

At this point the story took a strange turn. A magistrate from the Manchester area where Frank was now living heard about his case, and on investigating it was so convinced of Frank's innocence that she offered him a place to stay while instigating an appeal.

In the interim a film crew was recording Frank's story and in one memorable interview after two months of enforced exile, Frank broke down in distress at missing his family. Real men might not eat quiche but Yorkshire miners don't cry readily in public.

Eventually the appeal succeeded and the charge was dropped, at which point I became involved in recording Frank's homecoming. We filmed him at home with his family and then down at his local club surrounded by relatives, friends and well-wishers, the scenes uncannily reminiscent of the climax to that perennial Christmas film, *It's a Wonderful Life*.

In the wealth of events during the year-long strike, there were probably many such tales from both sides of the dispute. One could just as easily have done a sympathetic

piece about a police constable injured by loutish pickets.
However the film made it clear that wherever one's
sympathies lay, it was misleading to hang mass labels on
individuals, to dub all miners as bolshy and violent, all
police as corrupt and excessive. On such a broad stage all
types would be playing their part.

If you lost any money during the '87 stock market crash I
have to confess to actually being there to watch it disappear
down the gurgler. I would have tried to stop it for you, but
my knowledge of futures and securities is a trifle limited. If
the price of pork bellies goes down I might buy a couple of
chops for the weekend, but that's about the limit of my
financial acumen.

I was due to work on what looked like being a deeply
unmoving programme, a documentary about one of the
investment banks in central London. It seemed fairly routine,
likely to be of interest solely to the financial community, and
was destined for a Sunday afternoon slot some six months
later. I knew that there would be the standard shots of
dealers talking into three phones at the same time, plus
interviews with high-powered financial wizards all speaking
a language only slightly more comprehensible than Serbo-
Croat.

So we turned up at the bank's headquarters on the
morning of Monday, 19th October, 1987 (cue opening bars
of *Jaws*).

The first meeting of the morning confirmed that this was
going to be no ordinary start to the week. The New York
market had suffered a bad Friday, dropping over 230 points,
and it was clear that investors were looking to sell. What
was not clear and what nobody could have predicted was the
wild, abandoned free-for-all that was about to occur.

We started off in the dealing rooms with some of the
city's Young Turks, who daily negotiate deals for mind-
bogglingly large amounts of the folding stuff. In one day a
dealer might conduct $500 million worth of business, with
every phone conversation being recorded to resolve any later

disputes. Earning commission on sums like that made one begin to understand how someone in their twenties could make £250,000 a year. The lifestyles of such high flyers had risen above the mundane materialism of flash cars, mews flats and country cottages to embrace the seriously expensive world of art collecting.

But today's pickings were not going offer so much as a 'Blue Lady' print from Woolies. As the morning progressed, the scale of the crash became apparent with the 'Footsie', the Financial Times-Stock Exchange Index (the average share value of the top one hundred companies) dropping over two hundred points, when normally it might fall just ten or fifteen over a whole day. Panic selling had set in, creating yet more panic and the dealers seemed punch-drunk. Strained faces and heads in hands signalled the realisation that the gravy train of the past few years had not merely screeched to a halt, but had plunged headlong into the ravine.

Oddly enough, some dealers seemed almost light-headed as the nightmare unfolded, spouting 'Bye-bye Britain' quips as fall after fall taunted them from their screens. Being powerless to halt the market's downward spiral, perhaps they were revelling in the awfulness of this moment of financial history.

When the New York stock exchange opened in the afternoon it went into an immediate nose dive, killing off any faint hopes that perhaps the crisis could be contained within Europe. By the time Tokyo opened with the same result, it barely raised an eyebrow. The market collapse had become one of the biggest crashes since the war.

The crisis meeting at the bank the following morning was woefully lacking in adequate superlatives. Indeed the only phrase that began to capture the magnitude of what had happened was crude and wonderfully simple.

'Well, yesterday the shit really hit the fan.'

Now that kind of financial language I can understand. The sense of fear and gloom that pervaded the meeting was not because of one exceptionally bad day, but because the crash was simply the beginning, with repercussions that would be felt for several years.

So, hands up anyone who wants to buy shares in a luxury goods company. This, unbelievably, was the challenge now facing the bank as several weeks earlier they had undertaken to mastermind the public sale of the Paris fashion giant, Yves St Laurent, and the flotation date was now a mere three weeks away. Your mission, should you decide to accept it....

We flew to Paris with two of the bank's Top Guns to cover a crisis meeting with the YSL board. It seemed fairly pointless, as no-one was going to buy into a high fashion and perfume company when expensive consumer items are the first to suffer in a recession. Eventually both sides agreed that the sole option was to sit tight and wait for better times. It was to be another two years before YSL finally became a public company.

Back in London the financial gurus tried to analyse what had happened. The previous year had seen 'Big Bang' (the computerisation of financial markets and twenty-four hour worldwide trading), which had spawned a new breed of whizz-kid dealers, complete with cellphones and portable faxes but lacking the traditional years of carefully acquired financial acumen.

Add to that share-dealing computers that automatically sell or buy when a stock price hits a certain mark and you had a volatile mixture waiting to explode. A period of soaring prices had created the inevitability of an eventual fall and when the first dip appeared, the computers kicked in with a selling spree that quickly spread worldwide and snowballed out of control. The new kids on the block were caught napping and by the time the world's central banks were able to react it was too late to stop the rot.

In total contradiction to my initial expectations it had been a fascinating week. Not only had I been witness to a moment in history, but I had also developed a new respect for the larger-than-life characters who daily juggle sums of money that exceed the imagination (on the wall of the managing director's office was a framed cheque for £500 million - um, could you put your name and address on the back please?)

The programme's graveyard slot was quickly brought forward to prime-time when the producer touted the hottest film in town. Broadcast as *The Money Slaves* the film ended with the stark fact that the crash had resulted in worldwide losses approaching $1 trillion (that's $1,000,000,000,000!)

And the name of the company who made the film?

World's End Productions.

To date I have no experience of pregnancy or childbirth, either personal or vicarious (apart from my own birth of course, but my recollections of that are a little hazy). So when I was booked to work on a documentary about foetal surgery I reckoned I was about to be chucked into the deep end of the learning pool.

The King's College Hospital in southeast London was one of the first in the world to offer this amazing surgical treatment of foetal abnormalities. Given that a foetus may be just three or four inches long, performing surgery on what would be tiny bladders and kidneys seemed challenging beyond belief. And it was all the more amazing how casually the operation was carried out.

We arrived at the hospital fully expecting to have to go into operating-theatre mode i.e. donning the *MASH* greens and wiping all our equipment down with disinfectant. But the surgery was a low-key affair, performed by just one specialist and assisting nurse in a small room off one of the wards.

In the corridor outside, a number of pregnant women were waiting their turn. Having started to faint during the one time I tried to give blood ('No, it's no good, we won't be taking any from you - don't worry, it happens to a lot of men'), I was full of admiration for the young women who were swapping pregnancy tales with apparently no sign of nerves about their approaching experience.

Once inside the operating room, the patient's abdomen was scanned with an ultrasonic device to provide an electronic image of the foetus in the womb. Having worked on a few medical programmes, I'd seen the ultrascan in action, but to me the results always looked like a high-pressure front coming in over the Atlantic.

After identifying the problem area, the specialist inserted two probes into the anaesthetised abdomen. These allowed the procedure to be carried out by remote control guided by the fuzzy image on the screen. The surgeon deftly wielded the probes while casually explaining what he was doing to the equally casual expectant mother. I've had worse times at the dentist. Moreover, both parties seemed oblivious of the gawking film crew merely inches away. I certainly wouldn't be so amenable if someone was poking a camera at me while I was trying to work or having....um.... intimate surgery.

The whole process didn't seem to take more than about fifteen minutes, and by the third patient I'd become as blasé as the participants. The medical miracle I was witnessing was not only rectifying existing problems but also often preventing possible miscarriages. I imagined the child-to-be later viewing a recording of themselves being operated on as a foetus. Now that's what I call a home movie.

Perhaps the most delicate aspect of documentaries is the temporary intimacy between subject and film-maker. After entering people's lives, recording personal moments and perhaps becoming quite close, we up and leave and rarely ever see them again. Then the following week it's the same with someone else.

After we left John, our Tourette's subject, he apparently went into severe depression, having briefly enjoyed for once being the centre of attention but not mockery. Then we were gone, back to London and he was once more left to cope with his affliction. I never saw him again nor heard how he was managing but I wish him well.

Someday I'll get a proper job

Covering actual events you sometimes get to rub shoulders with the rich and famous and discover some vital piece of information - such as what is their favourite fish.

World in Action tends to steer clear of such controversial matters but not so Noel Edmonds' *Late Late Breakfast Show*. At the 1985 Conservative Party Conference, the mission was to buttonhole the party elite with this burning question and elicit an answer for an eager nation.

The tactics were pretty crude. None of your wimpish, 'Excuse me Mr Tebbit, we're from the BBC programme *Late Late Breakfast Show* and we were wondering....' Nope, just rush the victim and go for the jugular.

'Mr Howe, what's your favourite fish?'

'Mr Heseltine, what's your favourite fish?' Compelling stuff.

To their credit most of our victims played along and managed a straight reply without looking too stupid, but we met our match in Norman Tebbit, who simply grinned, 'Shark.'

The only exceptions to the good humour were Ted Heath, who cruised by ignoring us, and Jeffrey Archer, who was initially both defensive and aggressive.

'Who are you? What's all this about? Turn that camera off.'

We explained what we were doing and spotting an opportunity for a bit of PR, Archer turned on the smiles and the smarm as the camera rolled and we repeated the question.

'Ha ha ha, you're not going to catch me out, Noel Edmonds, my children have warned me about you ha ha ha.'

And some people call him insincere.

By mid-afternoon we had gained a few notable scalps, but still had yet to confront She Who Must Be Obeyed. Filing a formal request for an interview with the PM simply to discover whether she prefers cod or haddock had about as much chance as Ambridge hosting the Olympics. So we decided to tackle her head-on during one of her walkabouts around the conference centre.

When you see past shots of Mrs Thatcher pumping the flesh, you really have no idea of the chaos around her. The media rat pack is out in full force, with journalists, photographers and news crews from around the world all struggling to get that vital quote or shot. Pitted against them just off camera are the government minders, pushing back the hordes to give their leader a little space.

On this occasion scuffles broke out as rivals were shoved out of the way, sometimes to the ground, while La Stupenda cruised along, exchanging small-talk with carefully vetted bystanders.

Our chances of grabbing even a couple of seconds with Thatcher were looking pretty slim, when suddenly she turned and found herself face-to-face with our young director, out on her first assignment with the programme.

'MrsThatcherwhatsyourfavouritefish?' gabbled our incisive reporter.

Thatcher, who had been walking around sipping a cup of tea, spluttered slightly at the ludicrous question but quickly regained her composure.

'Ah, yes, my favourite fish, well, yes that would have to be cod but of course only North Sea cod.'

God, she was good. You could see the cogs whirring into action. Press Button B for patriotic spiel.

Perhaps relieved at the opportunity to get away from such trifling issues as unemployment and inflation, Thatcher warmed to the seafood theme.

'....and of course lobster's very nice but *(tilts head slightly to right, smiles weakly and adopts hushed sympathetic tones)* it is rather expensive.' Who said she was out of touch with we common folk?

On she went and after about thirty seconds I glanced around the assembled media. The battle-hardened news crews, their talents honed from Belfast and Beirut, were glancing at each other in desperation at this nonsense, wondering when they were going to get something decent to file for the *Six o'Clock News*. I could imagine frantic editors trying to cobble together something of newsworthy value.

'Today the Prime Minister, Mrs Thatcher, reaffirmed her position with Europe regarding Britain's North Sea fishing rights....'

A spoof ad for the army once read: 'Join the army, travel the world, meet new and interesting people - and kill them.' When making documentaries you can also meet new and interesting people....

Take, for instance, a certain independent film producer (and I'm being gracious in the description) who was making a documentary about a village on the North York Moors. He shall of course remain nameless, but for argument's sake let's call him Philip Day and the village.... ooh, well, let's call it Glaisdale.

The evening before the shoot, Andy (the cameraman) and I met Philip in the local pub. The long greasy hair, pallid complexion and battered anorak were a world away from the leather-jacketed trendies of the London producer scene.

'I'd buy you a drink but I'm a bit short of cash.'

I guess we should have smelt a rat there and then, but my faith in human nature assumed he'd just missed the bank that afternoon - and cash machines were a bit thin on the ground in Glaisdale.

Philip suddenly became all formal.

'Right, first thing we have to do is elect a union representative.'

This seemed a little strange. With a large crew on a feature film lasting several weeks, there would probably be a representative to sort out any difficulties that might arise over hours, working conditions and so on. But there were only three of us - and one of those was the producer - for a one-day job. Electing a union representative seemed a slight case of overkill for democracy and workers' rights.

Andy and I looked at each other.

'Well, we're not that bothered.'

'Got to have a union rep - I'll do it if you like.'

'Er, sure, ok.'

And so P. Day was duly proposed, seconded and unanimously voted to the post of BECTU representative for the crew being employed by Philip Day Films. I wondered how he was going to represent any problems we might have to the producer.

The next morning we headed off to Philip's house to do some interior shots. He was renting a run-down farmhouse deep in a valley and accessible only by a ten-minute drive down a dirt track.

As we approached the farm, the strains of a sixties icon came drifting over the fields.

The answer, my friend, is blowin' in the wind,
The answer is blowin' in the wind.

'Hey, Dylan, great!' beamed Andy, who knew every song Bob had ever written - and a few that he hadn't. 'He must be all right if he likes Dylan.'

We pulled up at the farmhouse to be assaulted by a decibel level that Woodstock would have envied. Philip appeared and indicated for us to come in.

Our eyes took some time to adjust to the darkness in the living room but our noses reacted instantly to the unmistakable odour of human vomit. Someone (can't imagine who) had thrown up in the corner of the room behind an armchair. And left it there.

We spent the morning in a surreal environment. Refusing to turn down the music, Philip had to mime each shot to Andy, whose face had now adopted a permanent wrinkle at the overpowering stench. Universal Studios it wasn't.

We finally staggered out of the house and climbed into Andy's Landrover to drive to the next location.

'Quite a character, isn't he?' laughed Andy, having seemingly adapted to the new concept of full-volume photography in glorious Smellaround.

'Sure, if you like listening to Dylan at a zillion decibels three weeks after he's thrown up.' No sense of the dramatic, that's my problem.

We wanted a panorama shot of the surrounding moors and so drove to one of the hilltops that overlooked the valley. With great ceremony Philip produced a compass and placed it carefully on the ground.

'That's the camera position.'

I placed the tripod and camera directly above the compass and viewed the endless countryside through the wide-angle lens.

Philip exploded.

'What do you think you're doing?' He knelt down on the grass and started jabbing his finger at the compass. 'I'm the director and when I give a camera position, that's where I expect it to be placed - there!'

I stood back and eyed the tripod; it was perhaps an inch out, totally irrelevant for such a wide shot. But then I'm not a great artiste - or a complete wacko.

This sudden outburst revealed Philip's true nature. One moment he would be calm and lucid and the next he would break into uncontrollable rage. We managed to complete the day without either Andy or myself being impaled (or impaling him) on the tripod and were grateful to see the back of him.

Predictably he never paid our invoices and a few months later disappeared, having run up several other debts in the area. We heard a rumour that he'd been receiving treatment for schizophrenia, which would have explained his violent mood swings.

So when it comes to meeting new and interesting people I sometimes wish I'd joined the army.

Working in public usually brings a film crew into contact with the police, as we tend to disrupt normal life with an array of vehicles and equipment. Generally clearances have been sought beforehand, permits obtained and the phrase, 'We're part of the film crew' usually deflects any official objections. Occasionally, however, we come unstuck.

I was working in Belfast on a documentary about design, in particular how the city's security problems were

influencing the layout of the new housing estates. We had
finished early at one location and decided to take a coffee
break before moving on to our next interview.

Parking in Belfast is as difficult as in any major city but
made worse by the threat of car bombs, which has greatly
reduced the spaces available. We drove around looking for a
space until eventually I spotted a small gap on the junction
of two streets. I was a bit dubious about parking on a corner
but there was nothing else available and we were only going
to be away for a few minutes. What harm could it be?

We returned to find the van surrounded by the RUC, all
rifles, flak jackets and nervous glances at the stack of cases
inside the van. The senior officer asked for the driver. I was
about to step forward, when the rest of the crew retired three
paces. Thanks guys. I found myself facing the formidable
authority of Belfast's finest.

I realised that I was only a clever comment away from a
ride in a Landrover and so adopted the submissive pose used
by David Attenborough in dealing with gorillas. I then spent
several uncomfortable minutes at the receiving end of some
stern admonishment about the security situation in the city.

Thankful to have got off so lightly I started to leave.

'Just one other thing.'

I turned, expecting a 'No-hard-feelings-mind-how-you-
go-enjoy-your-stay' type comment.

'Yir porking's abuzmal.'

They've got some way to go to reach 'Have a nice day'.

If you've ever been lucky (or unlucky) enough to witness a
'Mr Puniverse' contest, you'll have been regaled by young
men with sand in their faces, stripped down to their Marks
and Sparks to reveal what could only vaguely be described
as 'a physique'. This skinny breed is a world away from the
bodies beautiful in films and advertising and I have to
confess a sneaking admiration for these sinewy few who
blow a very British raspberry at the cult of the gym - but
you'd never catch me doing it.

Entering such a contest requires nerve. Entering one in Barnsley borders on the perverse. Filming one in Barnsley pushes voyeurism to new depths. Enter the *Late Late Breakfast Show* (notice any pattern here?) who wanted to record the Yorkshire Area Finals, to be held in a Barnsley nightclub. Glamour beyond my wildest dreams. The competition was merely part of an action-packed evening that also boasted searches to find Yorkshire's Mr Cool, Mr Poseur and Miss Strippogram. I began to appreciate the cultural heritage of a region that had spawned J. B. Priestly, W. H. Auden and Geoffrey Boycott.

The contestants for Mr Puniverse duly stripped off and took the stage. A famine of biblical proportions had seemingly descended upon Yorkshire but only now was the true horror revealed. This was scandalous. Where were the welfare services? Where was *World in Action*? Where was Bob Geldof?

To their credit, the competitors attempted manly poses as they struggled to raise nonexistent biceps, sinews or muscle groups of any description. Put them next to a body builder and you'd be looking for a new form of DNA. The contest was duly won by a young man who made me feel like Schwarzenegger but he left the stage to be mobbed by a group of female admirers. Some guys get all the luck.

The next two competitions, to discover Messieurs Poseur and Cool, saw a tasteful barrage of gold chains and mirrored sunglasses, although images slipped somewhat when they had to chat up one of the barmaids to demonstrate their suave conversational abilities. They didn't quite resort to, 'So, do you come here a lot like?' but it wasn't far off and they all failed to prise away any of Mr Puniverse's admirers, so I guess there is some justice in the world.

Inevitably the evening's grand finale was the Miss Strippogram contest, by the start of which the club's largely male clientele were well 'tanked oop'. The girls, wearing little more than a smile, mounted the stage to face a display of formation leering. We thought we'd get a few incisive comments from the patrons.

'Phwoor, pal, you don't get many of them t'pound.'

'She'd be a bit of an 'andful.'

'One thing's for sure, she'll never drown.'

The contestants lined up and we moved in for close-ups - well, you have to get close-ups for editing reasons'n'stuff.... As we tracked along the display of bosoms I tried to concentrate on what I was doing, where I was, who I was. The cameraman was whispering something. I leaned in to try and catch what he was saying:

'Soft, soft....'

I think he was referring to my focus settings but I've never been quite sure.

In a similar vein, a commercial for a rock music station was to be filmed in a strip club (yea, ok, it's a tough job but someone's got to do it). On arriving we were greeted by one of the evening's artistes, who teetered up in precariously high heels and a few strands of (what was supposed to represent) a costume.

'Ooh, have you come to film our lesbian act?'

You don't normally get that working for the BBC.

We filmed the girls doing their stuff while the audience tried to behave like a bunch of guys having a great time at a strip club, but the underlying atmosphere for all concerned was that of seen-it-all-before boredom.

At one point I leaned over to the cameraman.

'We're nearly out of film.'

'I don't care,' he replied, absorbed by the on-stage action and continued to follow the performance as the film ran out.

That probably didn't happen on *Ghandi*.

The most notable exponent of the *Candid Camera* school of television was Jeremy Beadle with his programme *Beadle's About*. I worked on several of the 'stings' and enjoyed the technical challenge of working with a hidden camera, sometimes only yards from the subject. While most of the stunts were harmless, they occasionally crossed the boundary between good-natured fun and malevolence - for example, I could never see what was clever or funny about demolishing a replica of someone's prized possession (new car, boat, etc.) and filming their distressed reaction. Which might explain why Beadle ended up being voted 'Most Hated Man in Britain'.

Generally the scams that worked best were the simple ones. The more ambitious the plan, the more likely it was to fail. One of the more extravagant stunts involved a Royal Navy Wessex helicopter and a couple of royal look-alikes.

The setup was in a small village near Bournemouth. A garage is rung up and asked to help with a vehicle that has broken down behind a local hotel. On arriving, the mechanic is faced with an enormous Navy helicopter sitting on the lawn and a distressed pilot who asks him to pretend to work on the craft until a Navy mechanic can get there. This is all to keep some Very Important Passengers happy, notably the Duke and Duchess of York.

We arrived on location at about eight in the morning. 'We' in this instance being a crew of about forty people in various vehicles all descending upon this small village. It seemed ludicrous to imagine that no-one had noticed our arrival.

We spent the morning constructing the set and hiding the cameras. (There are tricks for hiding cameras but my lips are sealed - although you could always try bribery.) After lunch the first of our three selected victims was phoned, but predictably the word had got out and as soon as he turned up he realised what was happening and left immediately.

Our second and third subjects were equally sussed, and although they went through the motions of looking at the chopper from a distance, they steadfastly refused to get embroiled in the play-acting. By now things were looking bleak, and it was more than likely the whole affair would turn out to be an expensive flop.

In desperation another garage was called at random and someone agreed to come out and inspect the 'vehicle'. Fortunately for the director's budget our latest punter swallowed the story whole. The 'pilot' was Beadle, heavily disguised in flight helmet and mask, and he led our helpful mechanic through a range of scenarios, including bowing and saluting to the royal couple, trying to 'push start' the Wessex (which is about the size of a small house) and persuading 'Fergie' to remove her tights for use as an emergency fanbelt - yes, well, she might.

When the truth was revealed our mechanic took it all in good spirit and a very expensive day for London Weekend Television was saved.

Over tea I got a chance to talk to the two look-alikes. 'Andrew' was a Sheffield newsagent who simply played the part for a bit of fun and spare cash, but 'Fergie' had leapt wholeheartedly into the role after winning a national look-alike contest. She had subsequently given up her job in publishing to become a full-time Fergie, even to the extent of sometimes requiring bodyguards. A strange sort of fame.

Incidentally, if ever you get caught by Beadle and fancy getting a bit of your own back, just look bemused when he removes his disguise and brings out the big mike and say, 'I'm sorry, but who are you?' It will really ruin his day.

We needed some aerial shots of Newcastle but the budget wasn't up to hiring a helicopter, so the producer decided to hire a hot-air balloon. Not as controllable as a helicopter, but the shots didn't have to be that specific, so a balloon seemed a cheaper and adequate substitute which also offered a more stable filming platform.

We gathered at the Town Moor, an expanse of open ground on the outskirts of Newcastle. The balloon stood inflated and ready for takeoff, bright red and magnificently large. The difficulty was deciding who was going on the flight. With only three spaces in the basket, two would be taken up by the pilot and the cameraman, leaving the third spot open to tender. We were all eager to go and a genuine balloon debate occurred between Charles (the director), Dave (the sound recordist) and me.

I started with an opening salvo across Dave's bows.

'Well, I don't see why you should go 'cos you've already been up in a balloon once.'

'Yes, but that was only thirty feet up - and it was still tethered to the ground. Hardly qualifies as flight experience. And anyway I need to record sound.'

'What sound?' asked Charles. 'I hadn't planned on using any sound.'

'Well, birds'n'stuff, you know, general atmos,' defended Dave, now on shaky ground.

'Rubbish,' replied Charles, 'all these shots are going to be under commentary. If you want any high-level atmos, you can go and climb that tower block over there.'

The prospect of a twenty-six floor building with the lifts out of order made Dave reconsider the need for sound.

And then there were two.

'Well, as director I should go so that I can tell Tom [the cameraman] what shots I need.'

'But he knows what shots you need - and anyway we can't control what direction we'll be going so he can only shoot what comes up.'

'But I'm the director - you're merely the camera assistant.'

'An essential cog in the machine, actually - who's going to reload the mags up there, help change lenses, filters, put on clapperboards, make shot notes?' Most of this, I knew, would probably be unnecessary but a little economy with the truth never goes amiss - ask any politician.

Charles finally admitted defeat - but with one condition.

'When you come back down, every time you mention the trip it's going to cost you fifty p.'

I quickly gathered up the equipment and loaded it into the balloon basket before Charles changed his mind.

The securing ropes were released and we started to ascend, Dave and Charles bidding me a cheery farewell with, 'You'll pay for this, you bastard.' Crew camaraderie - you can't beat it.

The speed and silence of the ascent caught me by surprise. It was like being in a high-speed open lift but with no apparent form of power. Hot air always rises, right? Proven technology. No worries.

Yea, right. We're in a flimsy open cockpit that at any moment is going to drop like a stone. We're all going to die.

At about three hundred feet the pilot opened the vent at the top of the balloon to halt our ascent. Having now spent several minutes not tumbling helplessly to earth, I relaxed slightly and began to take in our surroundings. The city lay stretched beneath us with a degree of detail you don't have time to see from a plane.

We began to drift towards the River Tyne and the industrial estates beyond. We took occasional shots but most of the trip was spent revelling in the new experience.

Being only a few hundred feet up we still had some contact with people on the ground. Faces would look up, smile and wave. When we glided over a housing estate, what seemed to be every kid in the district rushed out and chased after us, an airborne Hamelin Piper.

We left the city and moved out over the countryside. We had all our shots and now had to find a landing site. Easier said than done. Our first approach was aborted because of farm buildings and our second because of pylons. Lifting the balloon out of these descents had used up all our gas, so the next approach had to be right.

The pilot eyed a likely location and began releasing air from the vent. But he'd left our descent too late and we were heading straight for a dense wood.

I packed away the equipment and braced myself for landing. We came in just short of the trees, bounced twice and skidded to a halt, the basket toppling over at the last moment. There was virtually no wind so our return to earth couldn't have been gentler, but I could appreciate those scenes of windier landings when basket and occupants are dragged helplessly along the ground.

Charles and Dave had been travelling with the support crew, who now arrived to pack away the collapsing mass of nylon. As Charles approached, I sensed an opportunity to gloat that could not be missed and waved my cheque book at him.

'Shall I just make it out to "Cash"?'

His reply was unprintable.

Grandstand wanted a piece about Manchester United's attempt to win the Premiership. We needed a shot from the pitch of the crowd reacting to a United goal, but as we could hardly hang around on the pitch during the match we had to fake it before the game started.

We walked out onto the field about fifteen minutes before kick-off and headed towards the Stretford End. Show no fear.

Martin, our director, tried to persuade the crowd to leap into sudden ecstasy as if United had scored. The response, however, was a bit weak so he started making certain - how shall I say - dismissive gestures in an attempt to incite a more vigorous response.

I think certain directors should come with a Government Health Warning. Call me old-fashioned, but suggesting to a packed Stretford End that they might all be guilty of a form of self-abuse that could affect their eyesight was like inviting Hannibal Lechter over for a barbecue.

We did indeed get a reaction, but not one that could be used for daytime viewing. Our immediate health prospects were not looking particularly rosy when the mob was distracted by the arrival of the teams and we made a discreet withdrawal.

So much for *vox populi*.

The above may give the impression that this business is a bit of a lark. Sure, it's largely enjoyable and offers a challenging variety of experiences, but as with any job there are downsides.

For a start, job security. Forget it. Even if you are fortunate enough to be on the staff of a television company you can suddenly find yourself part of a 'restructuring programme' that leaves you and several colleagues out in the big bad world hustling for a buck. The days when a job with the BBC gave you security, a pension and a lifetime's free copies of *Radio Times* are well gone.

Most technicians are now either freelance or on short-term contracts and live from booking to booking. The phrase 'you're only as good as your last job' is painfully true and if you mess up with a particular company, you can probably kiss goodbye to ever working with them again - because there will be hordes of highly talented eager people just waiting to take your place.

Being freelance generally plays havoc with your social life. Few are in the fortunate position of being so much in demand that they can pick and choose when they work. Most grab whatever they can whenever they can, because they know there are going to be lean times when the phone doesn't ring. So any social plans always carry the proviso, 'as long as I'm not working'.

Financially, the amount you can earn in a day may seem high, but out of that lump sum you have to allow for tax, national insurance, private pension scheme, a raft of insurance policies (sickness, accident, equipment, public liability, private health), as well as saving for holidays. And if you own equipment or a commercial vehicle, maintenance costs and loan repayments will erode your daily fee even more.

The industry can be unforgiving. If you're booked on a job, you turn up, however ill you may be. None of this 'Call the office, dear, and tell them I won't be coming in today.' Do that once and you'll have all the time in the world to recover. When it comes to pure unadulterated fun, there's little to compare with an exterior night shoot in freezing rain with a lulu of a cold.

The same with working conditions: rain, sleet, snow, freezing temperatures, scorching sun, dust-storms, howling winds, fifteen-hour days - all have to be endured while working on board ship, up a mountain or in a helicopter. If you are a bad sailor, flyer or hate heights, go do something else. Boats offer the widest range of experiences, from the sublime to the ridiculous: you can either be cruising through a calm sea in glorious sunshine or struggling on a tossing deck in freezing temperatures with regular dousings of salt water. And at all times and in all conditions the gear has to be kept safe, dry and dust-free.

Looking back, I think the worst day of filming I've ever done was (oddly enough) on land and at sea level, on a derelict housing site in Hull in December: sub-zero temperatures, horizontal sleet and everywhere piles of broken glass, rubbish and rubble. At least no-one was shooting at us.

Which brings me to antagonism. Not everyone wants to be filmed. They may hurl abuse at you, block the lens, throw a punch, pull a knife or simply shoot you. Fortunately I've managed to avoid the last three but there are plenty of news crews who haven't - and not all of them have lived to tell the tale.

If you want to be really unpopular, take a camera on to the Ford estate on Merseyside. Dubbed 'the worst council estate in Britain' they are understandably fed-up with film crews turning up to do yet another expose about the level of crime and unemployment in the area. Trying to work while stopping the gear from being nicked was a new challenge. It was uncanny hearing a twelve-year old accurately list the value of every piece of equipment in our kit. At one point we were surrounded by a group of locals who didn't take too kindly to our presence and blocked the camera. In the end we were forced to make a tactical withdrawal to ensure the safety of the camera - and possibly ourselves.

And after all that, you may not even get paid - or at least not for several months. Rare is the experienced freelancer who has not had a run-in with some dodgy company that delays payment for months with a variety of excuses.

'We never received your invoice.'

'We posted the cheque weeks ago.'

'We've been waiting for you to call.' One accountant I know ticks your name every time you phone to enquire about payment, waiting until you've acquired ten ticks before coughing up - 'otherwise they can't be that desperate for the money'.

'Our accountant's been off sick but you should receive something next week.' Some accountants seem to be permanently at death's door.

'The cheque's being prepared' - an odd one this. No doubt deep in the heart of the Scandinavian forests a mighty pine is being felled, which will some day be transformed into your cheque.

And the eternal, 'The cheque's in the mail.' This has become such a cliché that it is quoted as one of the three great lies of the film industry, along with 'You'll be on the next' (referring to the next job) and 'Just one more shot, guys', which a devious director can string out for about two hours at the end of a long day.

So, there you have it, a taste of the ridiculous that passes for making a living. You may have noticed that most of the above occurred while working in the 'real' world of documentaries as opposed to the make-believe world of television commercials or drama. In the latter, because one is fabricating an artificial environment the bizarre does not seem out of place, indeed it is often the norm.

Consider the television commercial. Given that most last about thirty seconds and have a shelf-life of about three months, commercials must be one of the most intense concentrations of money, time, effort and creative input of any artistic endeavour. Client and agency can take months developing an idea, followed by weeks of planning by a production company organising crew, cast, equipment, set, wardrobe, transport, meals, accommodation, traffic control, filming access, permits, customs and visas. The shoot may last several weeks and involve flying around the world to unspoilt (and thus generally inaccessible) locations. And all this just to sell you a beer, soft drink, or pair of jeans.

To the outsider it must all seem wildly inappropriate, given the ephemeral impact of all that energy and money on the human condition. Hmm, tough choice - tackle famine in Africa or tell them about Diet Coke.

Yet for those involved, tiny details in a commercial can acquire enormous significance. When Iraq invaded Kuwait, I was working on a commercial for a new ice cream. Sure the news was important but what was *really* important was making sure that the new sauce topping flowed exactly the right way over the ridges of ice cream. Six months later when Desert Storm was launched and a potential nuclear holocaust loomed, it was a perfume commercial and the condensation on that spray can just isn't quite right.

Easy to take cheap shots at the advertising industry and I'm as guilty as anyone, because I help make the commercials and work hard to ensure that they look as good as possible. But occasionally I find it worthwhile taking a step back and asking the eternal question, 'What's it all about, mate?'

Someday I'll get a proper job.

What's in a name?

A what? That's the trouble with having an unusual job title. Whoever you're talking to suddenly becomes partially deaf.

'So what do you do then?'

'I'm a camera assistant.'

'A what?'

'A focus puller.'

'Sorry?'

'A clapper loader.' By now my stock of imaginary hats is running dangerously low.

'Umm.'

'A film technician.' A bit vague, like the Chairman of ICI saying he works in an office, but by this stage I'm grasping at straws.

'Ah.'

At this point a certain amount of light begins to appear at the end of the cerebral tunnel. The inquirer struggles to recollect various end-of-film credits that may have briefly caught their attention as they scrunched their way out through empty crisp packets and spilt popcorn.

'So, you're a sort of grip!' they declare triumphantly, obviously pleased with their grasp of the terminology.

'Well, not exactly.'

'The "best boy"?' Struggling in the dark.

'No, but my girlfriend thinks I am.' This joke always falls miserably flat.

'So what exactly is it that you do?'

By now I'm beginning to wish that I'd confessed to selling life insurance or real estate, as nothing is more certain of rapidly changing the conversation.

The job of camera assistant can vary enormously with the type of filming. At one end of the scale there is the multi-million-dollar feature film requiring an enormous crew, with personnel for every imaginable task (plus a few unimaginable ones - I'm still not sure what a 'Rough Inbetweener' does). At the other extreme is the documentary crew consisting of perhaps just two or three people, all trying very hard to blend into the wallpaper. In between you have commercials, music videos and television drama, all of which can vary from small, low-key affairs to vast, extravagantly crewed productions.

For feature films, television dramas and the larger commercials, the camera department alone can consist of five people for the main unit and crews of two or three for any additional cameras. Once an exclusively all-male club, the camera department now often includes women, but for the purposes of brevity I have used male pronouns in the following descriptions.

The director of photography

Also known more simply as the *cameraman*, or on British films as the *lighting cameraman* or the 'guvnor', or in America as the *director of cinematography*. (I always thought that referring to myself as 'Assistant Director of Cinematography' would be useful chat-up line at parties, but I never had the nerve to be quite that pretentious.)

The DoP is responsible for transferring the cinematic wishes of the director onto film. In the weeks of preproduction before the actual filming commences, the cameraman and director will work through the film. Each scene will be discussed, and sometimes individual shots, with regard to lighting, set, costume, soundtrack, film stock, choice of location and lens selection.

Once on set the cameraman is responsible for the composition and lighting of a shot i.e. the framing and the look of a shot. This requires both artistic sense, to be able to create the picture, and technical knowledge to light and shoot it. There are also the demanding intricacies of special effect shots, such as blue (or green) screen, where the subject is filmed against a blue or green backdrop and the resulting image transposed onto a separately-shot background.

On top of all this the cameraman must have managerial abilities to organise and lead a large crew of technicians and keep them working at maximum efficiency. Quite often he will be issuing instructions for the setting up of one shot while simultaneously discussing the next with the director.

The cameraman will be assisted by the *gaffer* and the *operator*. The gaffer is the chief electrician, who in turn has a first assistant (the *best boy* - there, now you know) and a crew of additional electricians (*sparks*). Once the cameraman has discussed the shot with the director, he will tell the gaffer what lights to rig and the operator what shot he wants.

The operator

To the casual observer the operator (often known in America as the *second cameraman*) seems to have the cushiest job on set: simply sitting behind the camera on the 'dolly' (the small wheeled camera platform used in moving shots) and pointing the camera at the actors when the director yells 'Action!' It looks like one of those classic 'I-could-do-that' jobs but only when, as with any difficult task, it is being done supremely well.

The operator is responsible for setting up the shot in accordance with the cameraman's instructions. This will involve decisions on camera position, lens selection, type of camera mount (which can vary from a simple tripod to cranes with remote control systems) and the precise framing of the picture. The actor's costume, personal appearance and make-up must also be checked, which can sometimes call for great tact. One camera operator I worked with had to ask an actor to trim the luxurious growth of nasal hair that was dominating the close-up shot.

Once the camera is rolling the operator not only has to follow the action but also check for any technical glitches, e.g. soft focus, microphones in shot or unwanted background objects, such as television aerials on a Victorian rooftop.

At the end of the shot the operator will instantly be assailed with questions, from the all-encompassing 'How was it?' to the tiniest detail: 'Could you see that fly in the background?' An instant judgement must be made, as the pressure to move on to the next shot is ever present. Everybody is grateful for a quick decision of approval, but nobody remembers having applied any pressure when the film is viewed the next day and some previously unnoticed detail makes the shot unusable.

With all these qualitative judgements to be made, it might seem that actually manipulating the camera is the least of the operator's problems. Not so. A large 35mm camera is fixed to a heavy support plate (the 'head') which is rotated ('panned') left or right, or tilted up or down by means of a gearing system controlled by two wheels, a mechanism possibly derived from old artillery guns. These wheels must be mastered to such a degree that the operator can move the camera in any direction without conscious thought, changing the speed and/or direction of one or both wheels simultaneously.

Thus to be a successful operator requires endless practice and a level of physical and mental dexterity equivalent to tossing pancakes with one hand and solving Rubik's cube with the other while riding the Mad Twister Roller Coaster - in the rain. But you try telling that to the young people of today....

The focus puller or first camera assistant

The *focus puller's* involvement with a major film can begin two weeks before filming starts with the checking and testing of the camera equipment. Location filming can be gruelling for the gear: torrents of salt water while onboard ship, the heat and sandstorms of a desert, the mud of a battlefield scene, the icy cold of the Antarctic, the humidity of rain forests or the vagaries of an English summer. All can cause havoc in a piece of precision engineering and so you must plan for them while preparing, fitting and checking protective casings and coverings that can resist excessive dirt, moisture, heat and cold.

Filming tests are then carried out, to check the equipment is working properly and allow the cameraman to select the combination of film stock, filters, lenses and processing that will give the right look for the film.

After all the preparation it is something of a relief to arrive at the location and start filming. The first shot is established and the camera set up. This may be a simple tripod shot, or from the dolly or crane, or a more ambitious shot that requires the camera to be mounted on a car, truck, helicopter, boat, plane, train, even skis - the possibilities are endless.

The focus puller's job is basically to ensure that the shot is in focus. This can require a blend of technical expertise (involving complex optical calculations) with an appreciation of the dramatic nature of a scene. The focus may change during a shot and any focus pulling (adjustment) must be sympathetic to the mood of the action and performed at exactly the right moment and speed.

Once the shot has been set up and rehearsed, filming can commence. A scene may require several attempts or 'takes' before the director is satisfied, as a take can be spoiled for any number of reasons: actors can forget lines or miss their marks (be in the wrong position), a microphone may dip into frame, part of the shot may be out of focus, the sound may be ruined by unwanted background noise, a special effect may go awry or the director may simply want another crack at a particularly dramatic scene.

With a good take completed, the crew will move on to the next shot and the whole process is repeated. This is the pattern for a shooting day, with each shot presenting a unique set of problems.

At the end of the 'day', which can be 10 p.m. or later, the assistant director calls out the welcome words, 'That's a wrap'. Back in the camera store the gear is cleaned and checked - this can take two hours if conditions have been particularly rough. So from picking up the first case in the morning to finally locking up the camera store can be a long day: fourteen hours and more is not unusual.

When jobs last several weeks it is easy to become so immersed in the filming that the outside world almost ceases to exist. The film *Awakenings* was made at the same time as the freedom movement was sweeping through Eastern Europe, yet the crew hardly noticed, even though some of them came from Eastern Bloc countries.

The clapper loader or second camera assistant

(Also known as 'Get-Us-A-Cuppa-Tea/Packet-Of-Fags/ My-Expenses.')

In the early days of film-making the *loader* or *clapper boy* (female camera assistants were unheard of) had a relatively limited role within the crew: load the one film stock into the magazines, unload the exposed film, put on the clapperboard at the beginning of the scene and generally act as teaboy and dogsbody to the rest of the camera and grips department.

Nowadays the job has become highly professional, with the loader expected to be familiar with a wide range of film stocks and almost as knowledgeable as the focus puller about the complexities of modern film gear. One of the latest cameras comes with its own notebook computer for entering special operating commands into the camera's on-board memory.

In preparing for a job the loader will assist the focus puller in the checking, testing and preparation of equipment. He will also be responsible for the vast quantities and variety of film stock that will be used during the production, ensuring its safe transport and storage at all times, often a daunting challenge given the perils of heat, humidity, physical damage and airport x-ray machines.

Once the job is up and running the loader's day begins with a call to the processing laboratory to get a report on the previous day's film. There may be problems with exposure, focus, scratches on the emulsion or dirt in the picture frame ('hairs in the gate'). The director may decide the shot is still usable, but a serious problem could involve a reshoot. If the cost of a reshoot is prohibitive then the scene may have to be put together without the offending shot.

Assuming no major dramas with the lab report, the loader helps put the equipment into the camera van, and on arrival at the location helps the focus puller set up the camera.

The loader's main responsibility is ensuring that there is sufficient film stock of the correct type available for each shot. This may sound simple enough, but there may be perhaps four or five different types of film. So on busy days the loader can be constantly juggling available magazines with requirements for different stocks and spending most of his time in the darkroom (film can only be loaded/unloaded in complete darkness).

Once a magazine has been used up, the film inside is unloaded back into the film can for sending to the processing lab. Considering the humble position of the loader in the crew pecking order, he actually has more potential than anyone for causing disaster. Exposing the film to light when unloading the magazine can wipe out half a day's work. I have heard tales of experienced loaders on the biggest productions seeing their careers flash before their eyes when they open the supposedly empty side of a magazine. They then spend a sleepless night waiting to hear from the lab if the picture area on the negative has been fogged. If so, all the scenes on the roll will have to be reshot - dangerous stunts, battles or the destruction of an entire set.

'Er, excuse me, Mr Selznick, that scene where we burnt down Atlanta....'

The other main duty of the loader is to identify each shot with the clapperboard (or 'slate'). The shot number is written on the slate in chalk and announced for the mike - 'Fifteen, take one'. The clapstick is then closed with a sharp 'smack'. This gives a sync point between the film and the soundtrack, allowing the editor to identify the scene and match up pictures and sound precisely.

Over the years there have been attempts to replace clapperboards with modern technology but the tradition largely remains, although the wooden slate and chalk have generally been replaced by more hi-tech materials.

The tradition also appears to be very popular with the public: it seems to evoke Hollywood and there are always people itching to have a go at 'putting on the slate'. Yet for such a seemingly simple task I've yet to see anyone get it right first time: they hold the slate upside down, out of shot or facing away from the camera, they obscure the board with their hands, or (best of all) they catch their fingers in the clapstick and the editor gets an 'Ow!' as a sync mark.

At the end of the day the loader will help the focus puller to break down the equipment and take it back to the camera store. Here all the exposed film is packaged and sent to the lab for processing. This material is known as 'rushes' or 'dailies' as it is rushed to the lab at the end of each day and processed and viewed as soon as possible.

Camera trainee

Largely there to relieve the loader of some of the more mundane aspects of the job, such as fetching tea and lugging equipment cases around, thus allowing the loader to stay with the camera. The trainee will also take over putting on the slate if the loader is busy in the darkroom.

Being the trainee is an excellent starting position and much sought after by aspiring entrants to the business.

The grip

The *grip* is responsible for setting up the camera mount and moving it if necessary during the shot. A camera mount can be a simple soft bag placed on the ground for low-level shots, a hi-hat (a sort of very low-level tripod), a standard tripod or a dolly. More adventurous shots may require a jib-arm (a counter-balanced arm allowing vertical movement of the camera between about two and seven feet), a crane (basically a larger version of the jib-arm) or a cherry-picker (a hydraulic lifting platform for high-level shots).

These are some of the conventional mounts, but the grip may be asked to place the camera in any conceivable position: on the side or bonnet of a car, on a cliff face, looking vertically down over the edge of a tall building, on a plane wing, on the front of a train, boat, helicopter - the only restriction is the grip's ingenuity (which is usually limitless).

If a tracking shot is called for and the camera has to travel along mounted on the dolly, the grip has to lay down rails. These must be perfectly level, even over rough ground or along the side of a hill.

The grip also bears a weighty responsibility for the safety of the crew. With a camera crew thirty feet up on a crane the correct counter-balance is crucial. A filming platform may have to be rigged near a cliff edge. A high-speed car chase may need the camera right in the thick of the action. In many cases the camera team place their lives in the hands of the grip.

Although the grip works hand-in-glove with the camera crew, he is a head of department in his own right. On a large shoot the senior, or 'key' grip will have a team of grips, classified by their individual roles, such as dolly grip. They tend to attract nicknames ('Bear', 'Poncho' or 'The Rat'), generally tell the best jokes around the camera and in location hotels can get embroiled in the more bizarre sexual adventures (or so they would have you believe).

This is a breakdown of the camera crew on a major production, but as I mentioned earlier there are many other types of production varying in scale and duration. A television drama is usually shot on 16mm rather than the 35mm standard for feature films; the equipment is smaller and lighter, and the numbers of cast and crew fewer than for a full feature. Documentaries need far less equipment, fewer crew and a far greater degree of flexibility and mobility.

As the crew diminishes in number, each person has a less clearly defined role, perhaps doubling or sometimes trebling up on their duties. So for a documentary the camera crew would consist of just the cameraman and an assistant. The cameraman would be both director of photography and operator and sometimes also gaffer, while the assistant would become focus puller/clapper loader and also grip. But obviously the scale of duties and amount of equipment would be less than for a major feature film: for example, a black lightproof changing bag is used instead of a darkroom for loading film.

So that's who does what in a camera crew. Hopefully this will make for more lucid (and profitable) conversations in the future.

'A what?'

'Look, there's this book you might like to buy....'

Getting started

The prize

'Wanted - young person to train for exciting and challenging career. Physically demanding duties, potentially dangerous and unpleasant working conditions, possible violence. Willing to work in rain, snow and sub-zero temperatures. Irregular hours, no job security, no sickness benefit, no holiday pay, no pension scheme, no fringe benefits. Salary negotiable but cannot be guaranteed.'

Well, there's always the Pick'n'Mix counter at Woolies.

Despite this admittedly pessimistic picture of what working in the industry can be like, the number of people who go to any lengths to break into the world of film and television continues to greatly exceed the number of jobs available. Day-to-day film work can involve long physically tiring days, lousy weather, no social or private life - and absolutely no glamour whatsoever. Nevertheless the lure is always there, offering different things to different people, from potential Spielbergs, Godards and Truffauts to those who have 'done a bit of video at school'.

The problem

The hardest part of working in film or television is landing the first job, convincing a producer to invest their limited funds in someone who combines little or no skill or experience with the potential to ruin the work of all those around them (e.g. the novice clapper loader). Hardly an alluring prospect. Consequently, trying to break into the industry can be a long, demoralising and extremely thrifty period in one's life. I spent two years trying to land that elusive first job, largely because I knew no-one and had little idea of what I was doing. I hope I can help you avoid the mistakes that I made and offer that vital tip to getting your foot in the door.

Most of the advice will relate to getting into the camera department as obviously that was my area. However, as the situation is equally difficult for all sections, any guidelines here should also hold true for someone trying to get into areas such as sound, lights, props and production.

I'll be dealing with companies and organisations based in London, as it's the centre of the UK film and television industry. While some of the major cities (Bristol, Cardiff, Leeds, Manchester, Newcastle, Glasgow) have regional television stations, they support only a few independent production companies whereas London boasts hundreds. Yet away from The Smoke competition for any vacancies will certainly be less intense, your living costs lower and the advice here is as applicable to Scunthorpe as to Soho.

Throughout I'll be referring to 'Useful Names and Addresses' as well as the bibliography, both at the end of this chapter.

To begin

There are several conventional means of entry into the industry, all offering varying degrees of training and work experience. Briefly they are:
- the BBC
- ITV companies
- FT2, the industry's own apprenticeship scheme
- colleges and film schools offering practical training in film, television, video and multimedia
- the various equipment and facilities hire companies that service the needs of the industry.

The BBC

The BBC used to produce all its own programmes, with huge numbers of people and extensive training programmes to supply skilled production and technical staff for the organisation. However throughout television there has been a shift away from in-house production to commissioning programmes from independent companies, thereby reducing staff numbers and, by extension, the need for trainees.

Nevertheless the BBC still runs courses in television production and broadcast journalism, and you may see the occasional trainee post advertised for other areas, but you can gauge how stiff the competition is when such a conservative organisation describes the entry requirements as 'tough'.

If you can't land a training post, there are occasional work experience placements (temporary attachments to a programme or department), but again the demand for such positions is described as 'extremely high'.

For an official view of the situation the BBC produces a booklet called *The Way In*, which explains the various departments and entry requirements. If you phone up the recruitment department (see 'Television Stations') they'll send you a free copy.

In all, I think I applied eight times for studio or film camera traineeships at BBC centres throughout the country. There is a rumour that the corporation looks favourably on repeated applications, as they show 'commitment', but I never got any further than a second interview, where I spent an uncomfortable thirty minutes in front of three people being chewed up and spat out in little bits. At the end of the interrogation, which included table thumping and shouting (from them, not me), I received an apology from the main interviewer for the harsh techniques that had been applied.

'We like to ask people questions that we know they won't be able to answer, just to see how they react under pressure.'

On reflection, I'm glad they didn't take me on, as my career has been far more diverse, and coping with rejections was good experience for the realities of freelance life. But notwithstanding the slightest whiff of sour grapes, the training you'll receive from the BBC will be excellent. If I haven't completely put you off from applying, here are some points to bear in mind:

• *Age*. They like 'em young - ideally, fresh out of sixth form or university.

• *Location*. Most jobs tend to be in London but there are the occasional posts in the regions. You will vastly improve your chances if you are initially prepared to work anywhere.

• *Image*. The BBC may no longer be the bastion of white middle-class conservatism, but they still require an image that will not ruffle too many feathers. So it might be a good idea to dig out the jacket and tie or nice sensible dress and hide your copy of *Class War*. I will leave it to you to decide whether the rumours of MI5 vetting are true.

• *Qualifications*. All departments require 'a good general education' with either academic qualifications or practical experience in related areas. The more you can offer, the better your chances.

• *Flexibility*. If you're having no luck landing a trainee position, then try for a job, any job. Generally it's far easier to move sideways once inside the BBC than it is to get there in the first place, as many openings are never advertised to the public but filled internally. However if you do apply for a different post, then be prepared for some stiff questioning at your interview about your change of career path.

'So Mr Hakin, now you want to work in the staff canteen....'

• *Patience*. The personnel department deals with about 100,000 applications a year, so processing may not be a swift affair. Reckon on about four weeks between each stage of your application.

Independent television

A few of the major ITV companies occasionally run training schemes for new entrants, but again they largely rely on freelance staff for their productions. Although ITV is generally regarded as being less 'stuffy' than the BBC, its standards are no less demanding, so adopt a similar approach when applying. The range of work may not be as broad as it would be with the BBC, but any professional training place should be grabbed with both hands. You can expand your horizons later.

For a list of ITV companies, see 'Television Stations'.

FT2

After a somewhat chequered and nepotistic past, training within the independent industry was rationalised with the founding of FT2 (Film & Television Freelance Training). This is an umbrella organisation created by various trade associations and broadcasters to provide technical training for entrants into the freelance sector.

FT2 offers a two-year apprenticeship for junior technical grades, with genuine work experience in all aspects of the industry. Students work on attachment to various productions for on-the-job training, supplemented by short technical courses at accredited colleges and training centres. During the first year trainees experience placements across all departments - camera, sound, grips, editing, production, art department, hair and make-up - but for the second year they specialise in just one area. There are no fees and during training a nominal wage is paid plus some expenses.

With only some twelve places a year available and over 600 applicants you get an instant taste of exactly how tough this business can be. Unlike the BBC or larger film schools no formal qualifications or extensive experience are necessary, but the requirements are still high. To quote the prospectus: 'Candidates are expected to display a keen commitment to the industry, good communication and interpersonal skills, an ability to cope with the technical aspects inherent in many film and television jobs and, most importantly, a clear appreciation of the demands that will be placed on them should they eventually enter the industry'. Phew. I never knew I had all that.

In addition to the main scheme, FT2 also runs apprenticeships for researchers and those involved in building and painting sets (setcrafts).

For details of FT2 see 'Industry Organisations'.

Training colleges and film schools

While full-time film schools are fairly rare, there is now a plethora of colleges offering training in video. For a comprehensive list of courses available, the best guide is the annual BFI (British Film Institute) *Film & Television Handbook* (see the bibliography), which also gives an extensive review of the industry over the past year. But if all you want is information on courses, this is available in another BFI publication, *Media Courses UK*.

Most courses last two or three years and you may be able to get a grant from your local education authority. Otherwise you could consult the *Directory of Grant-Making Trusts* at your local library for organisations that give discretionary grants (see the bibliography).

You may notice that some schools and colleges claim accreditation by the industry trade union, BECTU (the Broadcasting Entertainment and Cinematograph Technicians Union). This is misleading: BECTU's predecessor, the ACTT (Association of Cinematograph and Television Technicians), used to recognise certain courses but BECTU has never officially done so.

Similarly misleading are courses that imply an NVQ (National Vocational Qualification) on completion. Naughty naughty. An NVQ is a recognised standard of skill and knowledge but it can only be gained vocationally, in other words through assessment by an examiner when you're in professional employment. While certain courses cover areas relevant to particular NVQs, one cannot acquire an NVQ simply by completing a period of training, however practical it may be.

However some of the video/television courses have been awarded accreditation by the Moving Image Society (formerly BKSTS, British Kinematograph Sound and Television Society) for their content, standard of teaching and practical relevance (see 'Video/Television Courses'). The film and television industry training co-ordinating body, Skillset, has considered an accreditation system for full-time courses but this has yet to materialise.

The country's two leading film courses are run by the National and the London International Film Schools. If you are considering applying to either, you should bear in mind the following.

The course at the National lasts three years, starting each January, and you specialise in one subject for the entire duration. Entrance is extremely tough as the school boasts an international reputation, attracting budding film-makers from all over the world. The prospectus makes it clear that the course is really intended for the more mature student, perhaps those in their mid-twenties, as you will be very much working on your own. Fees are not covered by the education authorities but the school offers a career development loan to meet tuition costs, in addition to a bursary for living expenses.

The grounds and buildings might appear a little rough, being housed in an old airfield base, but the hangers have been converted to large excellent sound stages and the facilities are more extensive than any other training establishment can offer.

Furthermore, the budget for your final project will be quite handsome, and by combining it with those of perhaps two other students, you can finance fairly major projects. If the thought of commuting daily to the Beaconsfield location is off-putting, the school runs a minibus service from central London.

The London International Film School is more conveniently located in central London, but obviously it does not have the same amount of space as the National and occasionally hires outside studios. Students are expected to work in all areas of film-making rather than one specialisation, and new entrants are accepted at the beginning of each of the three academic terms. Fees and living expenses are eligible for local education funding but the authorities tend not to look too favourably on private schools such as this.

When choosing a film course, ensure that it is devoted to practical film-making, as opposed to an academic study of the medium. (See 'Film Courses'.)

Facilities houses

I have to be a bit careful here. If you were to phone up one of the major camera hire companies and ask them about their training scheme for camera assistants, you would probably receive very short shrift. They take a dim view of people who join them as a trainee camera technician, are taught everything about the equipment and then disappear off into the industry just as the company is about to reap the benefits of its investment. So if you approach them, best be discreet about your ambitions.

Nevertheless, if you want to learn about the technical side of cameras there is no better place than somewhere like Panavision. After working there for a few years you should be familiar with virtually every piece of camera equipment that exists, and while that doesn't automatically make you a good camera assistant, it's a heck of a start.

Moreover, if you do leave to go freelance you should be able to repair most camera problems on site, be the hero of the hour and probably, as the saying goes, 'be on the next' i.e. the next job, the Holy Grail of the freelance technician.

If you apply to Panavision as a trainee camera technician you'll be put on a waiting list, which is currently running at about two years. Then, if you're really lucky, you might be taken on as post person for about six months until a vacancy occurs further up the ladder. You then progress to loading and unloading equipment from the camera trucks, and from there gradually work through the various grades of qualified camera technician. The whole process takes about seven years and is geared towards the school leaver (rather than someone in their twenties, as I was when I first started hustling).

As with the BBC, you could try gaining entry by other means, such as driving or office work, but there is no guarantee that you could then switch over to the camera department. So think carefully before you go for that job as Conveniences Maintenance Engineer.

With regard to other hire companies, the larger outfits like Joe Dunton's or Technovision may occasionally take on a trainee, but generally they are looking for experienced personnel whom they can let loose on equipment almost immediately.

See 'Film Camera Equipment Hire Companies'.

(All of the above relates to companies hiring out camera equipment, but the same will probably apply to firms supplying lighting and grip equipment, or any facilities area of the industry.)

So those are the standard options for breaking into the industry. I recommend you also look at a useful handbook called *A Career in Film, Broadcast, Video And Multimedia*, published by Skillset. The booklet gives a very clear, down-to-earth view of the industry, the jobs, the training and the skills, qualities and qualifications you are going to need to make it in the business. Copies should be available in your local careers library or you can get one directly from Skillset (see 'Industry Organisations').

But what if....?

All the above training possibilities may sound promising, but they are vastly oversubscribed. So what do you do if you've tried to get in through the training front door only have it continually slammed in your face? Where next? For the majority of aspiring directors, cameramen, editors and such like, the only option is to get out there and hustle hustle hustle.

Whenever I ask someone how they got their first break, they invariably start by saying, 'Well, I was lucky....' And whenever anyone asks me the same question I have to give the same reply. I was lucky - eventually - because I phoned a particular person at a particular time when they were looking for someone. One week earlier or later and I would have received the usual polite rejection. However I got lucky only after two years of being unlucky, of writing letters, making calls, slogging round companies and replying to ads, all to no avail.

The simple truth is that outside the conventional training options there is no right or wrong way to get in. What works for one person one day may never work again for anyone else. Even if one approach doesn't lead anywhere itself, it may lead to another path that leads to another that leads to another that eventually arrives at the right door. And if anybody or anything offers the merest hint of a job, never let them sleep. To adapt an old sales mantra, 'If they snooze, you lose'.

By far the best way into the industry is to be born into it. If your father/mother/brother/ sister/second cousin twice removed already works in the business they can open doors for you that would otherwise remain firmly shut. As they have already established their professional credibility, then in vouching for you some of that rubs off, and you can find yourself meeting people who normally you'd be lucky to get through to on the phone. Work experience and trainee positions materialise before your very eyes and before you know it, you're up and running and into your next feature. Having to enter life with the appropriate surname can prove a little tricky of course, but basically if you've got it, flaunt it.

The next best thing to a family contact is any personal contact in the industry. Even if they are not in a position to help you themselves, they will probably be able to pass you on to someone else. Being able to say, 'David Puttnam told me to give you a ring' again sets you above the common herd.

Getting experience

But let's assume that you have no family contacts, or in fact no contacts at all. Let's assume the worst possible scenario. Let's assume that you are me a few years back. Where to begin?

Well, for a start it's pointless going looking for work if you've got nothing to offer. Production companies are inundated with young people trying for that vital first break, but what a company is initially looking for is commitment, something that shows that you have a genuine desire to work in the industry.

While you may not have any professional experience, there are several areas that can offer the chance to gain knowledge and demonstrate that commitment:

- short courses
- personal projects
- workshops
- student films

Short courses

Short courses can offer the simplest means of actually getting your hands on some gear, using it in anger and, most importantly, getting some of the stupid mistakes out of the way before you start for real. (Try to make as many mistakes as possible as this will cut down the number available to you later in professional life.)

When the video revolution first occurred, private courses materialised everywhere offering to teach the new skills that would lead to a lucrative lifestyle. While they certainly resulted in a lucrative lifestyle, it was usually for the training providers, who charged exorbitant fees but who generally had few or no teaching qualifications.

But now there is Skillset, which oversees the many courses on offer throughout the country. While they don't offer any training themselves, they have approved certain courses for established industry workers wishing to upgrade their skills and provided funding for them. But Skillset also publish guidelines for entry-level courses to help you select the most appropriate.

As with full-time tuition, some short courses offer training relevant to NVQs but to get the qualification you still have to prove yourself in the workplace.

For the full range available, Skillset and the BFI have published a catalogue called *A Listing of Short Courses in Media and Multimedia*, which categorises studies by subject and geographical location.

Generally any course run or approved by established organisations such as the RTS (Royal Television Society), NFS (National Film School), BBC, ITV, BFI, BECTU, GBCT (Guild of British Camera Technicians), BSC (British Society of Cinematographers), Kodak, Skillset or the NSCTP (National Short Courses Training Programme) should be fine. And while there may be many genuine private courses around, if you are coughing up several hundred pounds in fees then you are entitled to ask some pretty direct questions:

• Does the course have any validation or accreditation?
• Is the course relevant to any NVQs?
• How many students in a class?
• How long are the teaching days?
• What equipment is available?
• How many practical exercises will you do and how much time will you spend directing, shooting, editing, etc.?
• Will everyone get the chance to direct, shoot, edit etc. on their own or do they have to share the job with another student?
• How many teaching personnel are there and what are their qualifications?
• What are the names of past students? Are any working in the industry?
• Will you receive a certificate or showreel on completion?
• Does the course give any help towards finding a job?

The more time you spend doing practical exercises, the more ambitious the exercises and the less sharing you have to do, the more useful the course will be. Unfortunately it's also likely to cost more, although there are bargains to be found at local colleges. I spent three weeks at South Thames College in Wandsworth on a television studio production course, which apart from being excellent experience was also incredibly cheap (£1 a week!) as I qualified for one of the subsidised places for the unemployed. With the changes in education funding, such deals may be no more but certainly check out your local college.

Personal projects

Apart from the knowledge gained, a course will put you in touch with like-minded people with whom you can perhaps start your own group project. After completing a short 16mm film course with Crosswinds, a private film school now sadly defunct, I teamed up with a fellow student and we spent four months devising, scripting, shooting and editing a short promotional film for The British Decorators Association! (It didn't do too well at Cannes, I must admit.) We shot on a clockwork 16mm Bolex and looking back on it now, it's as rough as hell, but it was a film - our film - and not only did our client order extra copies, but the following year asked if we could update it. In my books, a successful production.

Your choice of shooting medium will depend on what gear you can lay your hands on and the type of production you are planning. Video cameras can be hired relatively cheaply and with a domestic editing unit you can avoid expensive professional suites and edit your footage at home. Editing units can range from the relatively cheap and basic to the not-so-cheap and versatile with cuts, wipes, fades, titling and sound mixing. Check out the Data Video range at Highway Hi-Fi (see 'Film Industry Sales'). To save money, try hiring the camera and editing unit as a package.

As a vehicle for displaying your directing, writing, editing and camera skills, video is perfectly acceptable. However for superior image and artistic credibility, particularly when shooting drama, film is still the real

McCoy - even if it's just Super 8. You can hire a Super 8 camera through the London Film Makers Co-op, Four Corners Workshop or Lee's Cameras (see 'Film Camera Equipment Hire Companies'). For a guide to Super 8 in London consult *The Blue Corners Super 8 Film-maker's Guide*. Obviously if you can arrange to shoot 16mm with cheap gear (same companies again), short ends of stock (try the Film Stock Centre) and a cheap deal on processing (most labs will discount if you're flexible over times), then even better. Whether 16mm or 8mm, you'll have to be sparing with the film stock but editing is a breeze, with just a simple pic-sync and splicer.

For more advanced editing you can transfer your footage to video and use the units mentioned earlier, although transferring Super 8 to tape is somewhat specialised (try Telecine in London). But you'll end up with a showreel shot on film in an age when everybody and his dog seems to own a video camera and a wedding can resemble a White House press conference.

Workshops

There is no clear definition of a film or video workshop. Some will be no more than a collective of keen amateurs, paying an annual subscription for access to very basic equipment under the guidance of a tutor. Others may run cheap, intensive short courses in film and video-making, or organise community-based projects, but whatever their role they all offer advice and the opportunity to gain valuable experience.

A workshop will usually be run by one or two dedicated staff with a lot of amateur back-up, and may even offer the chance of a full or part-time position, albeit lowly paid.

In London the longest established film workshop is the London Film Makers Co-op. They have all the facilities for Super 8 and 16mm film-making and members can hire equipment well below normal commercial rates. Over the last few years, film and particularly video workshops have sprung up everywhere - for a comprehensive list refer to the BFI Handbook.

Student films

If you didn't manage to get a place on a full-time student course, you can still gain experience with them. All films are labour intensive and student productions can offer chances for keen and competent outsiders to get involved. Some National Film School productions in particular require fairly large crews and while the key positions such as camera will be taken by the regular students, there are usually vacancies in areas such as props, lights, set painting and sound.

Stick a postcard on the noticeboard of your local media school or college, giving your details and experience, and state in which area you would like to work, or - even better - that you are prepared to help in any capacity. Another pair of hands is always useful so I'd be surprised if you got no response. Obviously you won't get paid, but you may get help with fares and you will (or should) receive meals.

A word of warning: the people on such courses may, in the strict sense of the word, be amateurs but their attitude to the job will be professional and they will expect the same from you. Also the equipment may not be state-of-the-art, but it will be proper professional industry gear, extremely expensive and only to be handled by trained personnel. So the students will not take kindly to someone coming along and ruining their production through ignorance or incompetence, however keen or cheap they may be.

In other words, don't make yourself out to be something that you're not, or attempt tasks that you can't handle, because you will quickly be thrown off set if you start messing up. Be honest with people and they will fit you in accordingly and if you do alright, then you may get a chance to move up within the crew. After all, come the day when it is *your* production you will want a crew around you who can a) do the job and b) do it cheaply! (This is not always true in the professional world - some producers are more interested in price than performance.)

If you get known on the student circuit as someone willing and reliable, you should find yourself in fairly steady demand. You may never get a job of great responsibility (although on my first National Film School shoot I was boom swinger!) but it will give you a chance to observe, ask questions, make contacts and generally get a free education in film or video-making.

Getting your hands dirty

By the time you've explored all the above options, you may feel sufficiently confident to step out into the real world and try your luck. In departments not involving technical equipment I would say go for it, but if you want to work in camera, sound, grips or lights it is essential that you are familiar with professional equipment. (Note: to work in the lighting department you will need formal training as an electrician.)

While short courses and the like are great for introducing you to the basics of crew work, other than on student films it is unlikely that you will use top-line professional gear, so this is the next section of your learning curve.

Go back to the facilities companies who initially turned you down. With luck they'll remember you, and if you explain the extra experience you've gained and that you'd like to learn about the gear, then they will usually let you come in at a quiet time and go over a particular piece of equipment.

When I was first learning (you never actually stop learning) I used to spend days up at Samuelson's (later Sammy's and now Panavision), going over every bit of gear I could lay my hands on. I have to give thanks here to Guy Green and Barry Measure for allowing me access to cameras and equipment that must have been worth millions. Obviously the company will need to be confident that you're not going to damage anything, because they won't have the manpower to have someone looking over your shoulder at all times. This is where the knowledge I gained through my film course and work on student shoots stood me in good stead.

In addition to these days in the camera shop, I was also lucky enough to get on Samuelson's 'mini-apprenticeship' scheme. This gave me access to the camera department for two weeks, which could be spent either helping the staff check equipment going out on jobs, or going off into a quiet corner and examining the toys at leisure. Panavision now offers a similar basic one-week course to get aspiring camera assistants up and running, but in such a short time you can only learn the bare essentials, so you'll still need to put in the hours studying the gear on your own (see next section).

At the end of my two weeks I managed to wangle another week sitting in on camera tests for the feature film *Revolution*. The focus puller was Martin Hume, one of the Hume camera dynasty who seemed to make every major feature that came out of Britain. In between making lots of tea I saw how every piece of equipment is tested before going out on a major shoot. Again the crew were great and answered all my 'page one' questions with long-suffering patience.

Having already overstayed my welcome I stretched it out to another week in the camera shop, because it was Easter and they happened to be a bit short-staffed. So in all I had four weeks of intensive training in camera equipment and testing, and as a bonus received a written reference (and a limited edition sweatshirt!). Just shows what you can do with a bit of pushing.

Camera manuals

This section really is just for budding camera assistants, so if that's not your area you can skip this bit. But if you're one of the brother/sisterhood wanting to learn about the gear then read on.

A modern film camera is a complex and expensive piece of precision engineering and is not the kind of thing that you can pick up and go, 'Oh yea, that does that and this switch does this' - or at least not without danger of doing some damage. So to learn about the finer points you can either pester the staff technicians, which they will put up with for about ten minutes, or you can study a book on the camera and clear up any grey areas with the occasional question, which will usually be well received.

A camera assistant needs to be familiar with a wide range of cameras and so an authoritative reference work is invaluable. Most of the following should be available from the specialist or larger bookstores (see 'London Bookshops Specialising in Film and Television' and the bibliography).

My particular bible was (and still is on occasions) *The Professional Cameraman's Handbook* by Verne and Sylvia Carlson. My battered copy of the Third Edition has been supplemented by the equally excellent Fourth Edition, one of the few manuals to include the latest Arriflex 535. The book still covers many early models of standard cameras, along with a few less popular makes that you occasionally get thrown to cope with as a second camera.

I particularly like this guide, because it has lots of step-by-step plain English instructions, even down to which finger to use to remove a particularly tricky aperture plate from inside a camera.. Everything is backed up with clear photographs and idiot-proof sections entitled 'NOTE', 'WARNING' and 'CAUTION'. With this handbook you should be able to go over most cameras safely and acquire a good understanding of how they operate. Not cheap, but a must for learning.

Another close contender for the one book you must have if stuck on a desert island with a camera is David Samuelson's *Hands On - A Manual for Cinematographers*. With details on seventy different cameras, eighty magazine threading diagrams, maintenance tips and equipment checklists, it should see you through any situation and is a welcome update to his earlier publication, *Motion Picture*

Camera Data (although this did contain a chapter with the wonderful title 'What To Do When A Camera Is Dropped In Sea Water' - push the camera assistant overboard?)

For specialised guides to the modern Arriflex cameras there are three excellent publications by a New York-based cameraman called Jon Fauer: *The 16SR Book: A Guide to the System*, *ARRIFLEX 16SR3: The Book* and *The Arri 35 Book*. They have all become the definitive reference books for these workhorse cameras of the industry. Clearly illustrated and written in a comforting user-friendly style with a nice line in dry wit, all the books offer not just accepted camera lore, but endless in-the-field tips that only years of experience can provide. The SR3 manual can also be supplemented by three teaching videos to make the explanations even clearer.

Perhaps future editions will incorporate not only the latest models (and a more hard-wearing cover, please) but also the 765 camera, Arriflex's nod to the possible return of the 65mm format for feature film production after its heyday in the early sixties. Kenneth Branagh's *Hamlet* was made with the 765 and may point the way for other productions.

An equally excellent guide, this time to the Panaflex camera, is David Samuelson's *Panaflex Users Manual*. Yet another of his many contributions to Focal Press, this offers a nuts-and-bolts guide to the Panaflex system along with many useful 'how to' and 'whatever you do, don't do this' tips.

Finally, there is the famous *American Cinematographer Manual*, battered copies of which are in equipment bags all over the world. Although more of a reference work than a learning book it is nevertheless indispensable.

All the above are largely technical camera manuals, but the job of camera assistant is much broader than simply knowing how the camera works. A brilliant guide to the full scope of duties has been written by American camera assistant Fritz Hershey. Entitled *Optics and Focus for Camera Assistants*, the book explains the job in the finest detail while taking a Zen-like approach to becoming a professional film technician (there are ten pages on diet and exercise alone!) Essential reading for any budding camera assistant, it should also be compulsory skimming for all aspiring producers, so that they may grasp and appreciate the complexity of the job.

For details of all these books see the bibliography.

Hunting down the jobs

So now you've reached a point where you've amassed quite a bit of knowledge and experience. You can put the moment off no longer. Now is the time to go out and get yourself that first job. What follows is equally applicable whether you've been scrabbling around learning or have graduated from a period of formal training.

Before you start, it is important to be very clear exactly what kind of job you are going for. Early on I wasted time and effort applying for any and every vacancy, when often I was hopelessly unqualified for the post and sometimes not even that interested. It was only when I concentrated on trying to get work as a camera assistant that I began to get somewhere. If you yourself aren't even sure what you want to do, you can hardly expect a potential employer to take you seriously.

You might as well start your search with the vacancies advertised in the various trade papers and outlets. BECTU publish a weekly job vacancy list that is sent to members on Tuesday and made available to non-members on the following Friday on the noticeboard in the Union's offices in Soho.

If you have access to Ceefax, Teletext or the Internet, you can investigate a range of media job sites from the comfort of home. The BBC have a jobs page on Ceefax (696) as well as a website (www.bbc.co.uk/jobs). Similar sites are run by the Careers Service Unit (www.prospects.csu.man.ac.uk), the University of London (www.careers.lon.ac.uk) and the Guardian (www.recruitnet.guardian.co.uk), which also has an Early Bird service to keep job-seekers posted of all relevant vacancies by e-mail. Most large organisations will run websites listing vacancies.

Otherwise it is a case of ploughing through the many papers and journals that (sometimes) advertise jobs in film and television. A good reference library should take a reasonable selection but ideally try the BFI library in central London. If you fancy a little light reading you might try the following:

- Guardian (Saturday and Monday)
- Independent (Sunday and Monday)
- Sunday Times/The Times (Thursday)
- London Evening Standard
- Observer
- Sunday Telegraph/Daily Telegraph (Thursday)
- Ariel (internal weekly BBC newspaper - try the reception desk at the nearest BBC office or the BFI library)
- Broadcast (weekly)
- Television (published monthly by Royal Television Society)
- Audio Visual (monthly)
- Campaign (weekly)
- Screen International (weekly)
- Stage and Television Today (weekly)
- Time Out (weekly)
- Sight and Sound (published monthly by BFI)
- Media Week

So that's your weekly ritual. I think it's important to realise that job hunting, particularly in something as loosely structured as the film industry, is a job in itself, and you have to discipline yourself to check all possibilities on a regular basis.

Once you've found a promising ad, it's a good idea to phone up before you apply to find out more about it and, if the conversation is going well, ask if you could visit for a few hours/days to observe. No-one gets turned down for a job because they're too keen.

The hustle

What if you've applied for all the advertised jobs and got nowhere? Try again next week - and the week after, and the week after that, and so on. If you haven't heard about a job you applied for two weeks ago, get on the phone and ask what is happening. There is a risk in continually pestering people, but remember it's the squeaky door that gets the oil.

In the meantime, you can also try and look for vacancies that are never advertised (the majority), but simply get filled by word of mouth or personal contacts. Cold-calling is a soul- destroying process and you have to approach it with a very positive attitude. Someone somewhere out there has a job for you. It might be the next call you make, it might not, but ultimately someone will say 'Yes!'

Before you can start looking you will need some sort of guide to point you in the right direction. There are various directories that list every company and individual connected with the film, video and television industry. The two most established guides are *Kays* and *Kemps*, but these have been supplemented by an unwieldy tome called *The Knowledge*. The BFI's annual handbook is also a useful source, but is not as expansive (or as expensive) as the others.

As these are quite specialised, you may have to track them down either via industry bookshops or directly from the publishers (see the bibliography). Given how much they cost (£18-£75), you may like to check them out first, which you could do at the BFI library.

There are actually job vacancies everywhere: in production companies, studios, facilities houses, transport and construction companies. Everybody seems to need an assistant: directors, producers, editors, cameramen, grips, lighting gaffers, sound recordists, wardrobe supervisors, make-up artists, location managers, researchers, production managers, carpenters and painters. Unfortunately any vacancy is usually filled internally or by recommendation, so by the time you get to hear about it, it has already gone. So you have to try and pre-empt that situation by making contact just as the vacancy arises.

Scan the trade press, see who's moving where, which new companies are forming. A move means a vacancy. Network like crazy, use all your contacts from courses, workshops, facilities companies, anywhere. Build up a file of who's doing what, where and when. Have some cheap business cards made up and hand them out to everyone, telling them what you've done and what you're looking for.

When you approach someone for work, be direct. People in the industry are continually being pestered by hopeful entrants and haven't got the time for casual conversation. I practised brevity to the point where I could explain who I was, what I'd done and what I wanted in one brief sentence. Get the job first - the chit-chat can come later.

Clearly define your target. Only approach the people who are in a direct position to give you a job. For example, if you are looking for work as a camera assistant then you may have some success by calling up lots of directors, but they generally do not decide who gets the job. For a feature film the clapper loader is usually chosen by the focus puller, for a commercial by the production company and for a documentary by the cameraman.

If there are no vacancies then ask if you can attend the shoot simply to watch from a learning point of view. Valid though this may be, it is also a good ruse for getting on set, and once there you have a golden opportunity to make yourself useful as an extra pair of hands. Alternatively, you can offer to work for nothing, just for the experience. The danger with this is that you will always be seen by the company as someone who will work for free and not really a professional worthy of payment. Also, if you take unpaid work you may not be regarded as an employee and therefore not covered by employment protection or health and safety laws. But it's all experience and competition for jobs is such that companies can be selective about whom they choose to work for nothing.

How to approach companies was a subject of much debate among my fellow hustlers. Phoning is by far the quickest and easiest but it can become very expensive. Also there is little personal contact, you are easy to get rid of and once the receiver has been replaced, you're history.

There's also the problem of getting through to the person who can give you work. Unless it's a small company, this won't be the person who answers the phone. So don't say why you are calling but simply ask to speak to, say, the production manager, using their name if possible. This, however, can come unstuck if the receptionist puts you on hold to talk to the person in question, and then comes back with 'I'm sorry, but who are you?'

The next approach is to write to everybody first. Very time-consuming, expensive and exhausting, but it does allow you to present yourself in the best possible light and in a more permanent form. With e-mail the same can be achieved for a fraction of the cost, time and effort. Having written to a company you can then call up and say, 'I wrote to you last week....' i.e. you are someone, you already exist.

What kind of impact your letter makes will depend largely upon its form. The classic business letter is safe enough, but will make little impression unless your CV is outstanding. So it's likely to be destined for the bin or the depths of the filing cabinet or cyberspace, which amounts to the same thing.

Trying to be witty or zany is risky. It may pay off or - if you fail to tap into the reader's sense of humour - receive short shrift, but at least you'll have been noticed.

Then there is the bizarre letter, guaranteed to make an impact, which may even get you an invitation to the office, purely out of curiosity. People in the film industry are not your normal run-of-the-mill business community, and so you may get away with writing on a toilet roll, or a dustbin lid or (my favourite) sending a model 2CV car with a note saying, 'Here is my CV. If you wish to know more, then phone....' How can they resist?

The final approach is the direct hit, the foot-in-the-door-and-I'm-not-leaving-until-you-hear-me-out approach. This allows you to make personal contact and become a face to go with a name and CV. You are also more difficult to get rid of, and generally if you turn up with enough confidence and bravado and are prepared to wait around a bit, then someone will be dragged out to give you five minutes. If you have no luck on your first visit then at least they will (hopefully) remember you the next time you phone or call in. And the longer you hang around the premises, the more likely someone will find something for you to do.

Cold-calling in person, however, will involve a lot of time, travel and expense. And by just turning up on spec you may find that the company has moved, or that they are too busy to see you, or that the person you really need to see is out and could you call back later. In central London you will also have the challenge of getting past the security intercom, or worse still, standing in the middle of a busy street and shouting at someone leaning out of a window three floors up. To avoid all this you could try and make an appointment, but then you are back to merely being a person on the phone.

Obviously the best approach would encompass all three forms of attack: an initial letter, followed by a phone call and finally a personal visit; but if you are trying to hit every company, this will be very lengthy and expensive. Try concentrating on one small group, perhaps all those in the same geographical area. Hustle them until they either give you a job or refuse to talk to you, in which case you move on to the next batch.

As an aside, when you do finally get a job in whatever department, your first task will probably be to get the teas and coffees. Do not treat this assignment likely. Note everyone's preferences, right down to the type of sugar they want and don't make a mistake. If you can't get the teas and coffees right, no-one is going to trust you with more weighty matters. On the other hand, if you master this task and more, opportunities abound. I've chosen clapper loaders to assist me purely on their ability not to mess up mixing my Dry Martini....

A union man (or woman)

As soon as you've managed to get your foot in the door, consider joining the union. In the days of the closed-shop industry, the ACTT (the technicians' union) was the cause of much anger and frustration among aspiring entrants such as myself: to get a job you had to belong to the Union, but you couldn't join the union until you had a job. Made the Freemasons look like the Brownies.

How the tide has turned. Trade union legislation of the eighties killed off the closed shop, so jobs are now open to anyone and BECTU is virtually begging people to join in order to maintain its influence in the industry. All you need is evidence that you have worked professionally in the business - no more Catch 22, no more two-year probation, no more funny handshakes.

Yet for all its inequities, the old union system ensured that only those with sufficient skill and commitment were able to work in the industry. Promotion was a slow and controlled affair, resulting in experienced technicians who were regarded as among the best in the world. Indeed, many would bemoan the opening of the floodgates, which has allowed a whole new breed of untrained wannabees not just to enter the business but to rise with alarming rapidity to senior positions.

The majority of *bona fide* technicians belong to the union and membership still implies a degree of professional competence. The union also offers advice on job vacancies, insurance, tax, legal issues and working agreements, as well as producing a CD-ROM of freelance technicians for production companies. Looking for work doesn't stop after the first job. You'll need all the help you can get to obtain the second, so as soon as you've landed the first pay packet, get on the phone and join up.

Technicians' diary/message services

If you are working freelance then belonging to a diary service is almost essential. They take professional messages and bookings for jobs while you are busy working and impossible to contact. Furthermore, although strictly speaking they are not agents, they can also put you forward for work if a producer calls up looking for a cameraman/ sound recordist/make-up artist/whatever - so it pays to stay in their good books.

They usually charge a flat monthly fee. Some companies, however, work on commission on any jobs you do, but I found the flat fee simpler to operate, and less expensive if you happen to be getting a fair bit of work.

The established companies tend to have waiting lists, so try signing up with a new service that is looking for clients. Usually a diary service is not interested in inexperienced newcomers, so get some work behind you before you approach them.

New services are springing up all the time; for a list look in the current edition of one of the industry directories.

The future

So that's it, my totally unofficial, no-guarantees guide to getting started in the film or television industry. If having to hustle for work is off-putting, I would say don't even think about this business, because that aspect never completely disappears. Several years down the line you'll probably still be making the calls.

'Hi, Richard Hakin here, I've just finished a job and was wondering what you've got coming up - fancy a drink?'

Useful names and addresses

Television Stations

BBC Television
Television Centre, Wood Lane, London W12 7RJ
0181-743 8000

BBC Recruitment
Room 404, Threshold House, 65-69 Shepherds Bush Green,
London W12 8TX
PO Box 7000, London W12 8GJ
0181-225 9874/5/6

British Sky Broadcasting (BSkyB)
Grant Way, Isleworth, Middlesex TW7 5QD
0171-705 3000

ITV Network
200 Grays Inn Road, London WC1X 8HF
0171-843-8000

Anglia Television
Anglia House, Norwich NR1 3JG
01603-615151

Carlton UK Broadcasting
101 Saint Martin's Lane, London WC2N 4AZ
0171-240 4000

Central Television
Central Court, Gas Street, Birmingham B1 2JT
0121-643 9898

Channel 4 Television
124 Horseferry Road, London SW1P 2TX
0171-396 4444

Channel 5 Broadcasting
22 Long Acre, London WC2E 9LY
0345-050505

Channel Television
La Pouquelaye, St Helier, Jersey JE1 3ZD
01534-816816

GMTV (Good Morning Television)
London Television Centre, Upper Ground, London SE1 9TT
0171-827 7000

Grampian Television
Queen's Cross, Aberdeen AB15 2XJ
01224-846846

Granada Television
Quay Street, Manchester M60 9EA
0161-832 7211

HTV
Culverhouse Cross, Cardiff CF5 6XJ
01222-590590

Independent Television News
200 Gray's Inn Road, London WC1X 8XZ
0171-833 3000

London Weekend Television
Upper Ground, London SE1 9LT
0171-620 1620

MTV Europe
Hawley Crescent, London NW1 8TT
0171-284 7777

Meridian Broadcasting
Northam, Southampton SQ14 0PZ
01703-222555

S4C
Parc Ty Glas, Llanishen, Cardiff CF4 5DU
01222-747444

Scottish Television
Cowcaddens, Glasgow G2 3PR
0141-300 3000

Tyne Tees Television
City Road, Newcastle-upon-Tyne NE1 2AL
0191-261 0181

Ulster Television
Havelock House, Ormeau Road, Belfast BT7 1EB
01232-328122

Westcountry Television
Western Wood Way, Langage Science Park, Plymouth
PL7 5BG
01752-333333

Yorkshire Television
Kirstall Road, Leeds LS3 1JS.
0113-243 8283

Film Camera Equipment Hire Companies

Aimimage Camera Company
Unit 5, St. Pancras Commercial Centre, 63 Pratt Street,
London NW1 0BY
0171-482 4340

Arri Media/Media Film Services
4-5 Airlinks, Spitfire Way, Heston, Hounslow, Middlesex
TW5 9NR
0181-573 2255

Axis Films
Post 47, Shepperton Studios, Studios Road, Shepperton,
Middlesex TW17 0QD
01932-572244

Camera Associates
Pinewood Studios, Pinewood Road, Iver Heath,
Buckinghamshire SL0 0NH
01753-631007

Camera Engineering
The Old Forge, Mill Green Lane, Hatfield, Herts AL9 5NZ
01707-258 999

Crystal Film and Video
50 Church Road, London NW10 9PY
0181-965 0769

Four Corners Film Workshop (Super 8 and 16mm)
113 Roman Road, London E2 0QN
0181-981 6111

Joe Dunton & Co.
Elstree Film Studios, Shenley Road, Borehamwood,
Hertfordshire WD6 1JG
0181-324 2311

Gorilla Grip Co. Ltd.
Unit 11, Smallbrook Business Centre, Waterloo Industrial
Estate, Bidford-on-Avon, Warwickshire B50 4JE
01789-778838

Lee's Cameras (Super 8 and 16mm)
281/282 High Holborn, London WC1V 7ER
0171-831 6060

London Film Makers Co-operative (Super 8 and 16mm)
The Lux Centre, 2-4 Hoxton Square, London N1 6NU
0171-684 0202

Movietech
7 Northfield Estate, Beresford Avenue, Wembley,
Middlesex HAO 1NW
0181-903 7311

Optex
20/26 Victoria Road, New Barnet, Herts EN4 9PF
0181-441-2199

Oxford Film and Video Makers
The Stables, North Place, Headington, Oxford OX3 9HY
01865-741682

Panavision
Metropolitan Centre, Bristol Road, Greenford, Middlesex
UB6 8GD
0181-839 7333

Panavision Grips

5-11 Taunton Rd, Metropolitan Centre, Greenford,
Middlesex UB6 8UQ
0181-578 2382
Shepperton Studios, Studios Road, Shepperton, Middlesex
TW17 0QD
01932-572609
Manchester Road, Bolton, Lancashire BL4 8ZL
01204-705794

Redapple

214 Epsom Rd, Merrow, Guildford, Surrey GU1 2RA
01483-455044

Richmond Film Services

The Old School, Park Lane, Richmond, Surrey TW9 2RA
0181-940 6077

Ronford Limited Camera Hire

Pinewood Studios, Pinewood Road, Iver, Bucks SL0 0NH
01753-651648

Sheffield Independent Film

5 Brown Street, Sheffield S1 2BS
0114-272 0304/0314

Technovision Cameras

Unit 4, St Margaret's Centre, Drummond Place,
Twickenham, Middlesex TW1 1JN
0181-891-5961

Video Film and Grip Company

8 Beresford Avenue, Wembley, Middlesex HA0 1QD.
0181-795 7000
Unit 9, Orchard St. Ind. Estate, Salford, Manchester M6 6FL
0161-745 8146
Cardiff Studios, Culver House Cross, Cardiff CF5 6XJ.
01222-599777.

Film Industry Sales

Arri (GB) Ltd
1-3 Airlinks, Spitfire Way, Heston, Middlesex TW5 9NR
0181-848-8881

dSam Ltd (film computer software)
7 Montagu Mews West, London W1H 1TF
0171-723 6562

Film Stock Centre
68-70 Wardour Street, London W1V 3HP
0171-494 2244

Highway Hi-Fi
318-324 Edgware Road, London W2 1DY
0171-723 5251

ICE Film Equipment Ltd
No.2 Bridge Wharf, 156 Caledonian Road, London N1 9UU
0171-278 0908

Kodak Ltd
PO Box 66, Station Rd, Hemel Hempstead, Herts HP1 1JU
01442-261122

Lee's Cameras (2nd hand Super 8 and 16mm)
281/282 High Holborn, London WC1V 7ER
0171-831 6060

Cinebuild
Studio House, Rita Road, London SW8 1JU
0171-582 8750

Optex
20/26 Victoria Road, New Barnet, Herts EN4 9PF
0181-441-2199

PEC Ltd
2-4 Dean Street, London W1V 5RN
0171-437 4633

Stanley Productions
147 Wardour Street, London W1V 3TB
0171-494 4545
0171-439 0311

Telecine
48 Charlotte Street, London W1P 1LX
0171-208 2200

The Widescreen Centre (professional Super 8 services)
48 Dorset Street, London W1H 3FH
0171-935 2580
18 Lady Bay Road, West Bridgford, Nottingham NG2 5BJ
01159-455459

London Bookshops Specialising in Film and Television

Cinema Bookshop
13-14 Great Russell Street, London WC1
0171-637 0206

Foyles
119 Charing Cross Road, London WC2
0171-437 5660

National Film Theatre Bookshop
South Bank, London SE1
0171-815 1343

Offstage Theatre and Film Bookshop
37 Chalk Farm Road, London NW1 8AL
0171-485 4996

Waterstone's Booksellers
121 Charing Cross Road, London WC2
0171-434 4291

Zwemmer
80 Charing Cross Road, London WC2
0171-240 4157

Industry Organisations

Broadcasting Entertainment and Cinematograph Technicians Union (BECTU)
111 Wardour Street, London W1V 4AY
0171-437 8506

British Film Institute (BFI)
21 Stephen Street, London W1P 1PL
0171-255 1444

The Moving Image Society (formerly British Kinematograph Sound and Television Society)
63-71 Victoria House, Vernon Place, London WC1B 4DF
0171-242 8400

FT2
Warwick House, Warwick Street, London W1R 5RA
0171-734 5141

Guild of British Camera Technicians
5-11 Taunton Road, Metropolitan Centre, Greenford,
Middlesex UB6 8UQ
0181-578 9243

Royal Television Society
Holborn Hall, 100 Gray's Inn Road, London WC1X 8AL
0171-430 1000

Skillset
2nd Floor, 91-101 Oxford Street, London W1R 1RA
0171-534 5300

Film Courses (full-time)

Bournemouth Institute of Art
Department of Film and Television, School of Media,
Wallisdown, Poole, Dorset BH12 5HH
01202-533011
BA Film and Animation Production

University of Bristol
Department of Drama, Cantocks Close, Woodlands Road,
Bristol BS8 1UP
0117-930 3030
MA/PgD in Film and Television Production

Edinburgh College of Art
School of Visual Communication, Lauriston Place,
Edinburgh EH3 9DF
0131-221 6138
BA (Hons) Film and Television

Gwent College of Higher Education
Newport School of Art and Design, Clarence Place,
Newport, Gwent NP9 0UW
01633-430088
BA (Hons) Film and Photography (Film and Video)

London College of Printing and Distributive Trades
Media School, Back Hill, Clerkenwell Road, EC1R 5EN
0171-514 6500
BA (Hons) Film and Video

The London Institute
Central St Martins College of Art and Design, School Of
Art, 107-109 Charing Cross Road, London WC2H 0DU
0171-753 9090
BA (Hons) Fine Art, Film and Video

London International Film School
Department F17, 24 Shelton Street, London WC2H 9HP
0171-836 9642
Diploma in Film Making

Napier University

Department of Photography, Film and Television,
61 Marchmont Road, Edinburgh EH9 1HU
0131-455 2487/0131-455 2604
BA (Hons) Photography, Film and Television

National Film and Television School

Beaconsfield Studios, Station Road, Beaconsfield, Bucks
HP9 1LG
01494-671234
NFTS Associateships in
Production
Direction (fiction, documentary or animation)
Cinematography
Screen writing
Editing
Screen Design, Screen Sound, Screen Music

Northern School of Film and Television

Leeds Metropolitan University, 2-8 Merrion Way, Leeds
LS2 8BT
0113-283 3193
PgD Film Production (fiction)

Plymouth College of Art and Design

School of Media Production, Tavistock Place, Plymouth,
Devon PL4 8AT
01752-203434
B/TEC HND Media Production

Royal College of Art

Department of Film and Television
School of the Moving Image, Kensington Gore, London
SW7 2EU
0171-584 5020
Cinematography
Design for Film and Television

Direction - Film and Television Drama
Documentary - Film and Television
Editing
Production
Sound Design

Sheffield Hallam University
Northern Media School, The Work Station, 15 Paternoster
Row, Sheffield S1 2BX
0114-272 0994
PgDip/MA Film and Television Documentary
PgDip/MA Film and Television Drama

Video/Television Courses (full-time and accredited by
The Moving Image Society/BKSTS)

Bournemouth University
Talbot Campus, Fern Barrow, Dorset BH12 5BB
01202-524111
PGDip/MA Video Production

Plymouth College of Art and Design
School of Media Production, Tavistock Place, Plymouth,
Devon PL4 8AT
01752-385960
HND Media Production (Film and Television Option)

Salisbury College
Southampton Road, Salisbury SP1 2LW
01722-323711
Post HND BIPPS Post Qualifying Examination (PQE)

Southampton Institute

East Park Terrace, Southampton SQ14 0YN
01703-319000
BSc. (Hons) Media Technology

South Thames College

Department of Design and Media, Wandsworth High Street,
London SW18 2PP
0181-918 7006
HNC Television Design
HNC Audio Visual Design

West Herts College

Hempstead Road, Watford, Herts WD1 3EZ
01923-257661
HND Media Production

Bibliography

Careers Advice

A Career in Film, Broadcast, Video and Multimedia
Skillset (1996)
2nd Floor, 91-101 Oxford Street, London W1R 1RA
0171-534 5300

The Way in - Job Opportunities in the BBC
BBC Recruitment Services,
PO Box 7000, London W12 8GJ
0181-225 9874/5/6

Lights, Camera, Action! Careers in Film, Television, Video
Josephine Langham (2nd edition, 1996)
BFI Publications, 21 Stephen Street, London W1P 1PL
0171-255 1444

A Listing of Short Courses in Media and Multimedia
Lavinia Orton
Skillset/BFI Pubs, 21 Stephen Street, London W1P 1PL
0171-255 1444

Media Courses UK
Lavinia Orton
BFI Publications, 21 Stephen Street, London W1P 1PL
0171-255 1444

Film and Television Handbook
British Film Institute (new edition each year)
BFI Publications, 21 Stephen Street, London W1P 1PL
0171-255 1444

Camera Manuals

American Cinematographer Manual
ASC Press, (7th edition, 1992)

The 16SR Book: A Guide to the System
Jon Fauer (1986)
Arriflex Corp., 1-3 Airlinks, Spitfire Way, Heston,
Middlesex TW5 9NR
0181-848-8881

Arriflex 16 SR3: The Book
Jon Fauer (1996)
Arriflex Corp., 1-3 Airlinks, Spitfire Way, Heston,
Middlesex TW5 9NR
0181-848-8881

The Arri 35 Book
Jon Fauer (1989)
Arriflex Corp., 1-3 Airlinks, Spitfire Way, Heston,
Middlesex TW5 9NR
0181-848-8881

Hands On - A Manual for Cinematographers
David Samuelson (2nd edition, 1998)
Focal Press c/o Butterworth-Heinemann, Linacre House,
Jordan Hill, Oxford OX2 8EJ
01865-310366

Motion Picture Camera Data
David Samuelson (1979)
Focal Press c/o Butterworth-Heinemann, Linacre House,
Jordan Hill, Oxford OX2 8EJ
01865-310366

Optics and Focus for Camera Assistants
Fritz Hershey (1996)
Focal Press c/o Butterworth-Heinemann, Linacre House,
Jordan Hill, Oxford OX2 8EJ
01865-310366

Panaflex Users Manual
David Samuelson (2nd edition, 1996)
Focal Press c/o Butterworth-Heinemann, Linacre House,
Jordan Hill, Oxford OX2 8EJ
01865-310366

The Professional Cameraman's Handbook
Verne and Silvia Carlson (4th edition, 1994)
Focal Press, Butterworth-Heinemann, Linacre House, Jordan
Hill, Oxford OX2 8EJ
01865-310366

Funding Bodies

The Directory of Grant-Making Trusts 1997-98
Charities Aid Foundation (15th edition, 1997)
Kings Hill, West Malling, Kent ME19 4TA
01732-520000

Industry Directories

Kay's European Production Manual
BL Kay Publishing (new edition each February)
Pinewood Studios, Pinewood Road, Iver Heath,
Bucks SL0 0NH
01753-651171

Kemp's Film TV & Video Handbook - UK edition
Cahners (new edition each August)
34-35 Newman Street, W1P 3PD
0171-637 3663

The Knowledge
Miller Freeman plc (new edition each April/May)
Riverbank House, Angel Lane, Tonbridge, Kent TN9 1SE
01732-362666

The Blue Corners Super 8 Film-maker's Guide
Otto Ltd, Publishing Dept, POB 17810, London N15 3WP
07020-909888

Miscellaneous

Money Into Light
John Boorman (1985)
Faber